Parameters

of

Popular Culture

Parameters of

Popular Culture

Marshall Fishwick

Bowling Green University Popular Press
Bowling Green, Ohio 43403

CONTENTS

PROLOGUE 1

PARAMETERS 8

WHALES 15

ROOTS 24

HEROES 30

POP PRINCE 40

CELEBRITIES 46

ICONS 52

ART 58

BACK COUNTRY 66

FAKELORE 76

MOSAICS 83

THEOLOGY 95

MYTHOLOGY 102

GLOBES 110

TWO WALTS 116

TWO WARS 126

BUTTONS 136

HEGEL IN HOLLYWOOD 143

NORTH STAR 156

FINAL STROLL 162

NOTES 167

In a democracy, the majority has the chain in
its hand.

> —Alexis de Tocqueville

My consumers, are they not my producers?

> —James Joyce

It's like riding a white horse on top
of the world!

> —Astronaut on Skylab II

PROLOGUE

We are meeting each other, and we recognize each other; we
know we are the traveling pioneers of the new age.

—Jonas Mekas

A new international style has emerged in the late twentieth century.

Far more pervasive and spontaneous than earlier ones (classical,
gothic, romantic, modern) it transcends national, class, language and
racial barriers. Students proclaim it in the streets of Paris, Prague,
New Delhi, and New York. Once it was gun boats that fired the
shots heard round the world. Now it is ping pong balls. After twenty
years of isolation from the world of instant communication, China
emerges in the 1970's through her table tennis team.

There is as yet no clear understanding, or even name, for the new
style. But we apply and examine labels, even when they are not
wholly adequate. Another name for the just-emerging phenomenon
is Popular Culture.

Included under that umbrella, as it is currently used, are those
works and events (both artistic and commercial) which are designed
for mass consumption and the taste of the majority. Entertainment
is the key, and money is the spur. The word "mass," linked to media
like television, radio, film, and records, is often carried over to the
audience. The tacit assumption is that popular (or mass) culture reflects the values and aspirations of Everyman.

Popular culture is often said to be rooted in folk culture: the inherited oral wisdom of the *folk* (Americans like the word *folks*) passed on not only in tales, songs, and dances, but in games, traditions, and manners. Folklore, itself a relative newcomer to the Academy, has developed categories, methods, and systems (one thinks of Stith Thompson's monumental work, for example) which make for a viable academic discipline. This cannot be said, alas, of popular culture.

Both folk and popular culture are often contrasted with private (high, elite) culture, produced by talented individuals who follow rules (say, for the sonnet or sonata) which both they and their audience know and respect. This work is "private" in that it implies a one-to-one relationship. John Milton, a great "private" artist, admitted he wrote "for the fit audience, though few." No one who sought wide "popular" appeal and influence would begin with such a goal.

This need not—must not—lead to abandonment of standards and precedents. The only pose more exasperating than despising all forms of popular culture is extolling them all. To an elitist critic, popular art never reaches the profundity and subtlety of "private" artists; by their standards, they are obviously right. Popular art says *relax*; private art says *stretch*. Popular art tends to be neither complicated nor profound; private art, to be both. Yet popular culture, with its many forms, reflects attitudes and anxieties of most people; sometimes it reflects them very well, indeed.

Who, after all, has the right to prescribe what is "good" or "great"? Aren't relativity and tolerance required in cultural as well as in moral or political judgments? Isn't it better that different cultural segments try to understand instead of condemn one another?

Endless bickering about mob taste, mass audiences, and elitism, Benjamin DeMott notes, has ranked as the most wasteful activity on the contemporary intellectual scene. Why not approach various aspects of our complex culture in terms "that focus, not alone on the gap between them, but rather on likenesses among the human activities that make folk, popular, and high culture possible?"[1]

The man carving a (folk) duck decoy may be watching a (popular) sporting event on the TV. The athlete entertaining him—and inspiring an elite story in the *New Yorker*—dreams of the off-season when he can carve duck decoys. The scientist may rush home to watch (popular) Marcus Welby, M.D. while the writer of that TV script studies (elite) records in medical journals. And which of them mix Charles Schultz and Picasso in their visual diet?

"High" and "serious" art imply unwarranted judgments. Who is to say what is "low" and "frivolous"? Painters called Wild Beasts (*les Fauves*) in one generation will become the Establishment later on. The "vulgar" music of the Beatles becomes "classic" a decade later. When is the folk saga en route to becoming the academically-acclaimed epic?

There is some of all these styles in each of us—in vastly different proportions, of course. I like to think of culture as a baseball in flight, spinning so that the different segments are part of one object:

The essays that follow represent my effort to make such a focus. They are all too limited by my personal vision; but even when we see only through a glass darkly we must share whatever vision and insight we have. I have not hesitated to be subjective and autobiographical.

The most remarkable thing about our culture (or any other) is not the multiple differences, but the way in which they somehow congeal and make a totality—a "way of life," to use the common cliche. Elements of folk culture, coming from the least educated and sophisticated, are fundamental and inexhaustible. All "absolute lines" between various cultural forms and levels are artificial.

Jazz, for instance, is often labeled "the great popular art form" of the last half century; but are not musicians like Benny Goodman and Louis Armstrong in every sense unique—as distinctive in their genre as any "classical" musician? And hasn't "pop art" analysis become one of the more esoteric forms of sophisticated criticism?

Reverse the argument. Haven't writers and artists who began with the smallest and most elite of followings come to have wide appeal and influence? Can anyone miss the influence of Piet Mondrian on cityscape architecture and shopgirl dress-fashions? And weren't many of the most "popular" literary tendencies, as exhibited in prose, art, and film, derived from no less formidable an intellect than James Joyce?

Born in 1882, Joyce was obsessed with innovation and barrier-breaking. His work is a commentary on the evolution of mankind from its heroic beginnings; the portrait of a whole civilization which has lost spiritual paternity. His dilemma is precisely that of the Pop artists; how to deal with the real and permanent, yet reflect our new age and environment. Old forms and traditions are dead and trite. There is no alternative except to seek new ones.

Just as language has been riddled and blunted, so have religious and ethical structures. The foundations of the old mythology have crumbled. Beowulf is as ridiculous as Batman.

Language cannot be dissociated from states of feeling. To be human is to have a language. To be "outside" is to be impotent. Hence Joyce seeks new words, and combination of old ones, to open up new channels of communication. He isn't playing with the English language; he's trying to salvage it.

Ulysses and *Finnegans Wake* are studies of the misadjustment of form and content, reflecting our age like a cracked mirror, ending up in a complete babble. Though it looks haphazard, the style is quite functional, carefully contrived. Pages of incidental satire, puns, and buffoonery anticipate Pop tricks of the 1960's. Joyce is forcing technique to comment; the style and the method evaluate the experience.

Of course Joyce never was, or will be, "popular" with a mass audience. But how has his imagination and perception filtered into

5

our functioning culture? How many have unwittingly carried forth
his revolution?

For popular culture is basically subversive; opposed to the
"high and mighty," the Upper Crust. Thousands of comic books
and cartoons show this. Pens of men like Al Capp and Art Buchwald
can prove mightier than the sword. They are, in the *best* sense of the
word, journalists, dealing with daily life, one day at a time. The very
word, scorned by many academics, is equated with trivial, ephemeral,
shallow. This need not be so—any more than the scholarly tomes
"written for the ages" and "to advance the cause of human knowledge" will necessarily be profound, lasting, deep. My own experience,
both as writer and reader of many such tomes, indicates that the
opposite is more apt to be true. The fact that Shakespeare wrote for
the pit, and knew "little Latin and less Greek," does not seem to
have blunted his influence over the centuries. Jesus' comment on the
Kingdom of Heaven may also hold for the long-term impact of various
parts of our contemporary culture: "The first shall be last and the
last shall be first."

Whether or not popular culture is a discipline, a branch of the
social sciences, a portion of the humanities, it is in some measurable
way a "movement." In the broadest and truest sense, men have
made and followed "popular" causes and formulae for centuries. In
the academic world, interest in "popular antiquities" and "popular
literature" goes back for generations; it was specifically to replace
those two terms that William Thomas coined the word "folklore" in
1846. A generation earlier the Grim brothers, Jacob and Wilhelm,
had collected popular *Fairy Tales* and opened up new horizons for
both literature and linguistics.

Thus the Popular Culture Association, *Journal*, and curricula
that surfaced in the late 1960's were a continuation, rather than a
launching, of inquiry. Their closest connections existed with the
American Studies movement. Intense self-examination in the 1930's
and world involvement in the 1940's produced dozens of books and
programs labeled American Studies, American Culture or American
Civilization.

"In order to function as model and leader for half the world,"

Robert Walker noted in 1958, "America has had to explain herself most thoroughly to herself and others."[2] Prominent post-World War II scholars were usually either in literature (Tremaine Mc-Dowell, Robert Spiller, Willard Thorp) or history (Ralph Gabriel, Merle Curti, David Potter). In 1948 Professor McDowell formulated a "first law of American Studies": to present the complex design of human experience within which the student should eventually find a fundamental unity.[3] The ideology was Whitmanesque, with heavy emphasis on patterns, relationships, and parallels.

There followed a series of discoveries and rediscoveries. (How had we missed Edward Taylor, Herman Melville, limners, functionalism? Why had we slighted the vernacular, humorists of the Old Southwest, jazz?) A "search for a methodology" began, built often on cultural anthropology with its broad cataloging mechanisms and comparative standards. The publication in 1952 of A. L. Kroeber and Clyde Kluckhohn's encyclopaedic *Culture: A Critical Review of Concepts and Definitions* widened the concern.

Other disciplines and avenues were explored, especially in the social sciences; symbolic and mythic meaning; value conceptions. Several scholars have documented these years when American Studies were in transition.[4]

Fluidity remained the key. Some praised this as an indication of the liveliness of the field. Others, like Alfred Kazin, labeled it "collective auto-analysis," which allowed "any enforced joining of the unjoinable." Those teaching and writing in the controversial field worked and hoped for better horizons. Writing in 1968, Robert Meredith found "signs of intensity and unity," while admitting that "theory and methodology are still adolescent and not completely under control."[5]

Absorbing (sometimes obsessing) as theory and methodology are, they will not be our central concern. I will argue, indeed, that too great a concern with Platonic abstractions produces not strength but sterility. Popular culture is people. Popular culture is *practice* and *event*-oriented—it leans not towards Plato but Aristotle—towards percept, not concept. So will I.

Abraham Lincoln called America "the last best hope of the

world." For many, beset by increasing tension, inflation, deception, and corruption, that hope seems to be fading. "It's been a terrible year!" blurted out Assistant Attorney General Henry E. Petersen on the televized Watergate Committee Hearings (August 8, 1973)—and millions silently agreed. And yet the very *fact* of the hearings, and the intensive self-scrutiny that resulted, was one of the healthiest mass movements of the century. "The Founding Fathers didn't make allowances for television," Senator Dole of Kansas pointed out. Neither did anyone else. But if Jefferson were right when he said, "Give the people light and they will find their way," no one could deny that the big lights were on all over the country and the culture.

The parameters of our culture are electrified, computerized, synchronized, televised. The results are incredible and unpredictable. So the question must be asked: how fares the people's culture—that is, popular culture—in the last quarter of the 20th century?

1. PARAMETERS

"Parameters: an arbitrary constant each of whose
values characterizes a member of a system . . ."

—Webster's *Dictionary*

Just what are the parameters of popular culture? Shall we begin
with a short, acceptable definition of "popular culture"? Impossible.
The words, considered either singly or jointly, seem like elastic bands
that stretch in many directions. There are 21 "definitions" of the
verb *pop* in the 1970 *Random House Dictionary*—to say nothing of
the noun, adjective, abbreviations, and link words (popcorn, pop-
eyed, popgun, etc.). The definition just given in our *Prologue* falls
apart when we try to draw the line between "aritistic" and "commercial," or when we try to define "mass." We can come to terms with
"mass media" or "mass production"; but just who is this "mass man"?
   "I have been looking for a 'mass man' for years," Professor A.
A. Berger admits. "Like the Abominable Snowman, he seems im-
possibly evasive. He is a conceptualization, a bugaboo to scare
people."[1]
   One recalls John Dewey's comment on the danger of putting
something in "public hands." He did not know any hands which
were not private, Dewey said; which did not belong to someone.
I. A. Richards' comments on best-sellers goes further in pointing
out the danger of drawing imaginary lines between categories of art
and objects:

8

> Exemplifying as they do the most general levels of
> attitude development, best-sellers are worthy of
> very close study. No theory of criticism is satisfac-
> tory which is not able to explain their side appeal.[2]

That popular culture is so unpopular with many academic
critics has not drawn from them, in their denunciations, a clear
definition or explanation of that which they scorn. Thus Benjamin
DeMott can dismiss Marshall McLuhan as "our new king of Popthink" without ever telling us just what Popthink is.

There are, of course, dominant ideas or points in the many
descriptions and attempted definitions of popular culture. "Pop"
usually means one of three things in contemporary usage:

1) New, faddish, "in." To be "popular" is to be
   "top ten," a pace-setter. (The operative word
   is ephemeral—in today, out tomorrow.)

2) Vernacular, folksy, earthy. To be "popular"
   is to by-pass the elite and appeal to the ordinary man who is rooted in real life. (One
   detects some reverse snobbism and anti-intel-
   lectualism here.)

3) Universal - electronic - instant. To be "popular" is to be plugged in, via film, television,
   tape. (Here the appeal is to technology and
   McLuhan's Age of Circuitry.)

Common denominators in the three meanings emerge. Pop is an un-
flinching look at the real world today; a fascination with and acceptance of our mechanized, trivialized, urbanized environment; a mirror
held up to life, full of motion and madness. It is rooted in new fac-
tors—physical and social mobility, mass production, abundance,
anxiety. Pop challenges conventional boundaries and eliminates
walls between art and non-art, high and low culture. What we confront is not so much a fixed definition as a fluid approach—Einstein's

answer to Aristotle.

What a long run *that* Greek genius had! The "beginning-middle-and-end" muzzle he clamped on Western art went largely unchallenged for 2,500 years. Aristotle's famous dicta, in addition to being platitudinous, raises more problems than it solves. Define *what* you mean by beginning, tell *how* you recognize the middle, and decree *why* one must stop, and everything stiffens up. Classicism becomes formalism. Rigor mortis sets in. You end uptight.

Enter a host of "rules" on how many acts make a play, how many columns a temple, how many tears a tragedy. This, young people are saying, will never do. Down with Aristotle, and the whole Establishment! In this sense, Pop is the revolutionary reaction to officialdom; the clown stressing the wonder and whimsy of life. From it comes the idea of substituting flower power for firepower-laughter for rhetoric-original for traditional.

Despite the stress on nowness and newness, Pop has a long, complex history. Not enough has been discovered and recorded about prior pop; what was "popular" in ancient Greece, Imperial Rome, medieval Europe, colonial Africa. There is still much to be done in piecing together American precedents. Emerson, we remember, asked us to "sit at the feet of the familiar, the low." His sometime gardener, Henry Thoreau, loved "the music of the telegraph wires." Walt Whitman shouted his barbaric yawp from the rooftops of the world, urging us to

> Unscrew the locks from the doors
>
> Unscrew the doors from their jambs.

"I am not a bit tamed," he bragged. "I too am untranslatable." So he posed, shouted poetry at the sea, rode on the Broadway horsecar, pounded the open road. As we shall see in a later chapter, his unique mixture of concrete and abstract, adoring and absurd, anticipated today's Pop Revolution.

Artists like Peto and Harnett did on canvas what Whitman did on paper; by 1910 men were painting ash cans long before the vogue for soup cans developed. Charlie Chaplin ate his boots in *The Gold Rush*. Marcel DuChamp exhibited a urinal over the signature "R. Mutt." Dada, futurism, surrealism, and art nouveau helped set the stage for pop. During the chaotic creative years of the new century F. R. Marinetti published the Futurist Manifesto (1909), documenting the obsession with speed, machines, and motion which many think is unique in the 1970's. The role of pioneering Italians (Gino Severini, Umberto Boccioni, Giogio Morandi, Antonio Sant'Elia, Alberto Savinio) has been vastly underestimated.[3] So has the role of illustrators, cartoonists, and graphic artists like Walt Disney, the figure who best deserves to be called "Father of Pop Culture." Born in the last year of the nineteenth century, he became interested in animated cartoons; in 1927, en route to Hollywood, he invented Mickey Mouse. Born and bred to live not on cheese but film, Mickey championed popstyle and won the heart of the world, under names like Michel Souris, Miguel Ratonocito, Miki Kuchi, and Mikki Hirri. He has a logic of his own, and achieves an illusion of independence from his technocrat-creators. Disney's impact will be the subject of closer analysis later on.

For most people sights and sounds penetrate quicker than words: the Pop Revolution is more visual than verbal. The mind is not so much a debating society as a picture gallery. Our icons are no longer in church but on the tube—the N.B.C. peacock, the C.B.S. Big Eye, the cliché-ridden ad. Classical rules are abandoned. Paintings move, movies stand still. Films are reel illusion, as real life nudges out fiction. Goodbye, Gutenberg. The mourning becomes electric, as the world itself is an art object.

Pop art has, in fact, led the parade. In no field does the word "international" apply better, for the inspiration is Oriental painting, African sculpture, prehistoric cave drawings, and the punch-holes of computers. Nothing is too old, too new, too obscure, too banal, too distant, too close for the everything-all-at-once style. All human history is part of the usable past; literally all the world's a stage and a resource center. Art is not so much a discipline as a scavenger hunt. Walls between disciplines, like national boundaries in a jet plane, become meaningless. Today's art schools teach not only painting and sculpting but also electronics, wiring, and glass blowing. In addition to (often instead of) oils and clay, artists use transformers, laser rays, mercury vapor and carbon filaments. The resulting art isn't content merely to hang on the wall or sit on the floor. It beeps, buzzes, and pops.

So does the new pop music. Using unorthodox key shifts, unequal phrase lengths, and electronic umph, it saturates as it satisfies. The Teeneybopper, our new-born king, steps into it anytime and starts to grind. The Afro-American contribution was enormous. The patron saints are the Beatles, who began the Group Rock in the early 1960's. Then Bob Dylan fused folk and rock; defined his generation with "Blowin' in the Wind" and wrote its anthem with "The Times They are a-Changing." In his rasping, haranguing voice Dylan was town crier for the young world. "I don't believe in anything," he says in his crypto-autobiography, *Don't Look Back.* "Why should I believe in anything? I don't see anything to believe in." Still there is something haunting and beautiful in such Dylan couplets as:

> All I really want to do
> Is baby to be friends with you.

"People talk about Negroes as if they were objects," Dylan has also noted. This concern with the Black man is another trademark of international change. Pop gives the formerly submerged and segregated peoples instant visibility. It links together the two-thirds of the human race who are colored—for the first time. "Say it loud, say it proud, I'm Black!" sings Jimi Brown—and the whole world hears him. Black Pop Culture is one of the potential weapons for world understanding and peace. Whether it will be used to create or to destroy remains to be seen. It is now, and will continue to be, a major ingredient in the New International Style.

This style supercedes ideology. I have never seen a group of young people enjoy pop music more, or respond more vigorously to it, than Poles attending summer conferences in Krakow and Poznan.

The new generation is no longer willing to die for communism, capitalism, or any other ism. Instead they want to be tuned in.

We should remember that when Lenin sparked the 1917 Revolution he shouted not only "Bolshevism!" but also "Electricity!" He turned on the light and shocked a backward peasantry into the Electric Age. By 1970 the whole world was wired for sound. Anyone who would lead must face the Big Light; must live or die by his "image." The nineteenth century took its toll on worker's bodies; the twentieth on their minds. In place of the illusion of progress is the illusion of technique. The abrasive process of rubbing information against information accelerates. Instead of simple sequence there is radical juxtaposition. Political science has become instant alchemy. "Don't *tell* us about politics. *Be* political."

In short, seek meaning through movement. From the trips to the frontier to the "trips" of hippiedom, Americans have followed this formula. Daniel Boone, Buffalo Bill, Teddy Roosevelt, Timothy Leary, and Matt Dillon went thataway. They took with them weapons of violence and seeds of the new style. Characters in novels by Cooper, London, Hemingway, and Bellow did too. We are the Huck Finns, not the Siddhartha. Instead of watching the river flow by, we cross it.

"Instant" intrigues us. Mom thaws out instant meals to supplement instant coffee, instant soup, and instant sex. "Nobody has time any more to start from scratch," Arlene Dahl claims in *Always Ask a Man.* "We can't wait for the coffee to perk, the soup to simmer, or physical attraction to grow into love. Who has time to waste on preliminaries these days? Besides, you can always switch to another brand."

Fed up with old brand newspapers and magazines, people are finding avant-garde publications like *Village Voice, Ramparts,* and *The Activist* fresh breezes in a smoggy culture. On a more scholarly level, the *Journal of Popular Culture* is making review essays on "Mission Impossible" and "Diana Ross and the Supremes' Greatest Hits" subjects for graduate seminars instead of magazines.[4] The significance of such ventures is stressed by Edgar Friedenberg:

> The new music, films and newspapers are not just
> hippie curiosities. They may be the only thing keep-
> ing American society from being taken in by its own
> cant and drowning as if in a cesspool.

They are part of the New International Style. Some of this
material is trivial, childish, faddish. American society remains, in
theory and in fact, a wilderness shared. Our waterfalls and Watergates are over-whelming. On we sail, probing the water, the land,
the society. Who knows if we shall ever catch up with Moby Dick;
or if, once we have done so, he will turn majestically and destroy
us all?

2. WHALES

There go the ships, and there is that leviathan.

—Psalm 104

I too have sought and found the whale—not like Ahab, in the distant Pacific, but down the street, on a siding of the local branch-line railroad.

I still remember it well, even though I was only six. Everyone knew about it, and everyone went. The whale had been washed ashore (some said in Greenland) and had ended up on a railroad flat-car that jolted from town to town. When we got to where it rested, there was a canvas wall around the long-dead leviathan. But a man was outside inviting you in—for a dime (he preferred "only a tenth of a dollar").

Blowing a week's allowance involved an agonizing decision. Was it worth two whole weeks of two-for-a-penny jawbreakers before school? Or a Hoot Gibson movie, with a serial and cartoon thrown in? Clutching the dime in my palmsweaty hand, I hesitated at the ticket booth. The barker pushed me in, where both the sight and smell of the whale were overwhelming.

That was my formal introduction to pay-as-you-go popular culture.

About that time I also began the Saturday morning movie-ritual at the Rialto where (also for one-tenth of a dollar) one saw Hoot Gibson hoot and fair damsels fare. Once in a while there was a horror

movie, but Mom kept us home if she heard about it. Quiet pervaded
the house when Dad tuned in Amos 'n Andy, or H. V. Kaltenborn
and the news. There were football games, Prom queens, and the
Mickey Mouse watch that didn't keep time. And there was a spectacular *Gone with the Wind* ball, at which our aging, balding Mayor
appeared as Rhett Butler.

All this was, of course, out of school—and the parameter of
what any of our teachers considered "education." For them it was
not Rhett Butler or Hoot Gibson, but Matthew Arnold who prevailed. They too thought culture was, or ought to be, "the study and
pursuit of perfection; and of perfection, as pursued by culture, beauty
and intelligence or, in other words, sweetness and light."[1]

Even if the words were hard to comprehend I knew just what
sweetness and light was—thanks to the picture on our parlor wall. A
family heirloom of sorts, it showed King Edward VII and Queen
Alexandra sitting on stiff-backed chairs in Windsor Palace Garden.
I can still see him in the mind's eye . . . adorned with top hat, frock
coat, and boutonniere; carrying a silver-headed cane. Her plush hat
is veiled and plumed. A frail parasol rests against her knee, a feather
boa droops casually over her chair. Behind her an avenue of trees,
prim as palace guards, reaches to infinity.

In such rooms, under such photographs, people discussed
"better" toys, playmates, words. No one was in doubt about "the
right side of the tracks." Everyone sought what Matthew Arnold
called the best that had been thought and said—at least in Western
Europe. If one could also burn with a gem-like flame, so much the
better.

For those who raised and educated me (not in railroad yards,
but school rooms), the note was one of "high seriousness." Girls
must become ladies; boys, gentlemen. To this end one followed the
code (at least on the surface). Cuss words had to wait for moments
behind the barn, and questionable books dwelt in eternal darkness
under pillows or acceptable books.

In due time one entered *the* University, which in that time and
place meant Virginia. In Charlottesville one joined a fraternity,
learned to dress well, and ended up (no matter what tailor he pre-

ferred) wearing the robes of Platonism—that *haute couture* of academia. Honor, Truth, and Beauty were the goals; English literature the acceptable major. Thus one became a Cavalier; gentleman; aristocrat; elitist. These were the parameters of my youth.

Since I first encountered Plato and philosophic idealism at the University, I have always regretted that those who did the introductions didn't reveal what Thomas Jefferson (who founded it) thought of Plato. Years later I ran across this by the Sage of Monticello:

> While wading through the whimsies, the puerilities, and unintelligible jargon of Plato, I laid the book down often to ask myself how it could have been that the world should have so long consented to such nonsense as this? His foggy mind is forever presenting the semblances of objects which, half seen through a mist, can be defined neither in form or dimensions.[2]

Sir, I agree.

But Plato had it all his way in those days. We turned our backs on Parmenideas: "The time will come when philosophy will not despise even the meanest things, even those of which the mention may provoke a smile." My mentors were Ortega Y. Gassett, warning that "the masses not only vulgarize and dehumanize but actually destroy art"; T. S. Eliot, whose *Definition of Culture* was narrow enough to exclude even Pooh-Bah; and Ezra Pound, hooked on Chinese ideograms and Mussolini. There was too that haughty English don, F. R. Leavis, who would later be echoed by Denys Thompson and Oxford dons. Closer to home, elitist Dwight McDonald insisted that homogenized popular art did not even have the theoretical possibility of being good. *Against the American Grain* enunciated his Law of Raspberry Jam—unless checked, the tepid ooze of Midcult will contaminate all civilization.

"Unremitting talk about the good is not only boring but usually inconsequential as well," Abraham Kaplan wrote in 1966. "Aesthetic theory that is preoccupied with artistic virtue is largely irrelevant both to artistic experience and to critical practice, confronted as they are with so much vice." But 20 years separated my college days and Kaplan's observation. During that time I concealed my interest in radio, movies, comics, and other items dear to the *hoi polloi.* When I boarded my first navy ship my duffel bag contained not only a copy of the *Bluejacket's Manual,* but the *Poems of Milton—* and Tillyard's comments on them.

That ship was a seagoing tug, the ATR 8. Shaped like a bloated sausage, it carried us back and forth between buoys outside New York harbor, patrolling for U-boats that never came, and keeping logs that no one ever read. No one is more isolated from events than a deck officer on a superannuated tugboat. There was plenty of time to read Milton—and any other author I could get my hands on. That is where I was in 1945.

Nineteen forty-five—what a year *that* was! The face of death was everywhere: 72 D-Days in the Pacific alone that year. World War II had become so vast and complicated that the machine seemed to be running itself. On July 16 the first atom bomb was dropped in New Mexico. Said Winston Churchill: "This is the second coming in wrath." On August 6 another bomb was dropped on Hiroshima. The pilot wrote in his log book, "My God!" What else was there to say?

The city was gone, and an era in human history, too. From now on no city or country could give answers to the great questions. Only humanity as a whole could do that. The culture of our times is the property of all mankind. The whole world is wired for sound, and everyone is a part of it.

Relativity and relatedness: these are the keys to the contemporary world. The criteria of absolute truth (not only in science but in morality) has been replaced by values of intensity. No one can distinguish the experimental from the eccentric, the sensitive from the neurotic, the significant from the silly. To be human is to be myopic. All of us, in and out of popular culture, get lost in the flux. "I'll never forget old What's-His-Name. . . ."

New "truth" has come so fast that old categories of thought and conduct (the "fixed points" of Cartesian thought) have lost their validity. Everyone is free to make his list of the half-dozen most consequential developments since 1945:

1. The success in using and the failure in controlling atomic energy.
2. The mastery, manipulation and abuse of nature.
3. The failure to master and manipulate human nature.
4. The linking of space and time into space-time, and space-travel.
5. The beginning of circuitry, which means also the end of ideology.
6. The youthquake.

These changes are all of a piece. Such phenomena as depth psychology, nuclear physics, Funk art, Keynesian economics, racial violence, miniskirts, soul, Motown, Rock, Vietnam, Kennedy Cult, Nielsen ratings, underground films, Watergate and Jesus Freaks are inter-related. These trademarks of our times and culture are planted deep—relativity and relatedness. They move in and out of our thoughts and our lives and set parameters.

Of course these things were not clear to me when the War ended. The ATR 8 was put in moth balls along with the navy blues; I turned once more to the tweedy university. At least this much was clear: I wanted to study America. The poet who had won my heart was Walt Whitman, with questions like this:

Who are you indeed who would talk or sing to America?

Have you studied out the land, its idiom and men?

Are you really of the whole People?

Have you vivified yourself from the maternity of these States?

Little did I dream that in graduate school I would "vivify my-self" by studying Old Norse, methodology, and amply footnoted monographs in *PMLA* and other scholarly journals. Instead of bring-ing me closer to "the whole People," the doctorate strengthened my elitist philosophy and Platonism. Outside the Yale library was a city that would soon seethe with violence and revolution; of that I knew and thought nothing. The America we studied was safely locked up in the stacks.

Teaching well-prepped lads in a "good" small college, I found a cordial reception for such Higher Learning. A moment of crisis came when Father-in-law gave us a television set. We had all heard the Dean, and many another sage, condemn the boob tube. So we relegated the vulgar image-maker to an upstairs bedroom. What did teaching American Studies have to do with watching television?

The answer which today seems so obvious did not cross my mind then. After all, I was an elitist who had chosen to live in the Ivy Tower. Some years later I would come to understand what Norman Podhoretz meant by "an eternal isolation . . . which ends finally in sterility, dissassociation, and mandarism."

This is not to say that some American scholars had not made notable efforts to study and understand the world people inhabit and relish. As early as 1915, Van Wyck Brooks drew highbrow-low-brow distinctions, and Gilbert Seldes had begun collecting material on *The Seven Lively Arts.* Seldes wanted to restore a good con-science to people who were enjoying silent movies and *Gasoline Alley* —"but with an uneasy feeling that they ought to be hearing Puccini and looking at the murals of Puvis de Chavennes." Folklorists col-lected popular material, but generally got only a toehold in univer-sities. Edmund Wilson, Lewis Mumford, and John Kouwenhoven opened new areas, centering on "the unselfconscious efforts of com-mon people to create satisfying patterns, not inspired by ancient tradition, but imposed by the driving energies of an unprecedented social structure."[3]   Sigfried Giedion showed that molded plywood forms which revolutionized 20th century elite art were conventional material for ferryboat seats in the 1870's; that certain highly ac-claimed Bauhaus designs had been standard equipment on American reapers and mowers since the 1850's. Some social scientists drew material from super markets, filling stations, and neon-lighted streets on which Everyman makes his contemporary pilgrimage.

Most interdisciplinary scholarship of this type met with icy disdain. The Big Thaw got under way in the Kennedy Years, affecting films, literature, politics, journalism, and finally the academic Establishment itself. Significantly, the heading "Popular Culture" didn't appear in *Reader's Guide* until 1960. The "silent generation" and the boot-licking "organization man" passed. Emphasis moved from silence to uproar; from negative to positive values; from turned off to tuned in. This recognition of inescapability, on a private and public level, moved modern thought from existentialism to social realism. (What ever happened to David Riesman's *Lonely Crowd?*)

More and more scholars came to recognize popular culture as a barometer, mirror, and monument of the world around them; the cutting edge of American Studies, expanding further the inquiry into and between subjects that began a generation ago. Those of us over 30 must acquire its idiom and flavor; those under have been unable to avoid this *lingua franca* of their generation. Popular culture is their culture, norm, mode. Perhaps we are not ex-elitists but post-elitists. Neat categories and barriers are disappearing. Hard becomes soft, drama becomes audience, small becomes large, silence becomes music. Men like John Cawelti are both fascinated and frightened by the new radical cultural transformations. "At times they seem to hold out the promise of a revitalization of our culture," he writes. "At other times I wonder whether it is not simply an evasion of cultural responsibility."[4] Meanwhile Peter Haertling, viewing the 1970 international Book Fair in Frankfurt, reported: "This has been a fair of pop singers, famous fliers, and obsolete comic strips. I suppose great novels are a thing of the past."[5]

Susan Sontag, who is *Against Interpretation,* also argues that the novel is dead. Interpretation is the revenge of the intellect upon art. "Even more, it is the revenge of the intellect upon the world." There are new standards of beauty, style, taste: pluralistic, high-speed, hectic. "From the vantage point of this new sensibility, the beauty of a machine, of a painting, of a film, and of the personalities and music of the Beatles is equally accessible."

When a field of study comes of age, it produces synthetic studies that show how the jigsaw puzzle can be assembled. Such a book was published in 1970—Russel B. Nye's 500-page volume (in Dial's "Two Centuries of American Life" series) *The Unembarrassed Muse: The Popular Arts in America.* Dealing with popular fiction, poetry, theater, art, heroes, music, and media, Nye set a new standard for comprehensiveness. He documents the gradual improvement over the years of popular standards of performance. The simple literalness of Tom Mix and Edward G. Robinson has become the symbolic, multileveled popular art of *High Noon* and *Bonnie and Clyde.*

Nye, who helped create the elite studies and attitudes which he now examines, spearheads the reevaluation of popular culture in modern critical thought. "To erase the boundaries created by snobbery and cultism," he writes in the final chapter, "that have so long divided the arts, means, in the long run, greater understanding of them."

Many others now try to find that greater understanding; to set sensible parameters. I do not want or intend to become a "specialist" in some tiny facet of popular culture studies. Already there are dozens (perhaps hundreds) of scholars who know more than I know—or want to know—about early phonograph records, late pornography, obscure films, pulps, campaign buttons, beer cans, Coca Cola memorabilia, and the "golden days" of radio, hula hoops, and flag-pole sitting. Their methods and materials range from ingenious to inane . . . one of the fascinating things about our whole enterprise. For every bona fide historian there are many bibliophiles, antiquarians, family-tree swingers, and propagandists.

The only thing that strikes me as more incredible than loathing all aspects of popular culture is loving them all. I stake my claim in the vast, ill-defined middle ground. One can learn from fads without falling prey to them; can enjoy the process while dismissing the product.

After all, nothing begins as "art" but as *something*—a picture, shelter, chair, cathedral. In the beginning is the function. "Art," the semantic label, is an afterthought.[6] Once art-objects exist, they find a place on a single line with two poles:

USE $\longleftarrow\!\!\!\longrightarrow$ AESTHETIC

Why then are some arts "fine" and others less so? Is a Picasso "finer" than an ax handle, if one is trying to survive on the frontier?

Speaking of frontiers: can we survive on the new frontiers of urban America? Can we understand the forces shaping our lives, then shape them to make survival possible? In seeking the parameters of popular culture, some answers—at least, some hints—might appear.

Seeking the "middle ground," in my own life and thought, has taken me into areas that are generally labelled elite, folk, popular. I am now convinced they are organically fused—part of my own cultural needs and personality. They form a verbal profile, and outline my parameters. I have nothing to offer except these fragments. Just as popular culture consists of thousands of individuals, so does my knowledge of it consist of many fragments or tesserae. As you will see in the chapters that follow, they have to do with heroes, celebrities, whales, roots, icons, fading regional memories, plane rides to Italy, echoes of Uncle Remus, snatches of college lectures on Plato. . . . I have been awed and amused by the Cardiff Giant, Ravenna mosaics, Disney Land. . . . Parallels between two Walts and two Wars intrigue me, as does Hegel's pendulum in Hollywood and McLuhan's pontificating in Canada.

Until very recently, I would not have admitted to this odd, irrational mixture—and would never have thought of concocting a book from it. Dealing with popular culture, on both personal and academic levels, has been a great liberating force, not only for me, but for my family and many of my friends. It has rejuvenated my teaching, and I hope my thinking. Perhaps the chapters that follow will give hints as to why this is so—and encourage others to follow the yellow brick road.

3. ROOTS

The land of the heart is the land of the West.

—George Pope Morris

These roots are very deep—into the landscape, landslides, and landfills that make any culture possible.

No one sensed this better than Ralph Waldo Emerson, who insisted that anyone who would understand America must first examine "the meal in the firkin; the milk in the pan; the ballad in the street; the news of the boat; the glance of the eye; the form and gait of the body." This sense of the earthy, the particular saturated the thought of William Byrd, Mark Twain, and many of the major writers who have followed in their wake.

People and that gritty substance called "entertainment" are interwoven, and interact in countless ways. It is the earth alone that man may touch, pat, smell, till—and upon which he lives, toils, dreams, and dies. In that earth are the roots.

"The utility, fruitage of life does not come from the top to the bottom, but like a great tree, from the soil up," Woodrow Wilson wrote in *The New Freedom* (1913). "A nation is as great, and only as great, as her rank and file. You cannot love a country if you do not have the true rootages of intimate affection which are the real sources of all that is strongest in human life."

These "roots of intimate affection" of which Wilson spoke are also the roots of popular culture.

24

Here we must beware of getting sentimental or unrealistic about the Virgin Land. Too many people who spend their lives typing, not plowing, have done that. The antidote is to study records or photographs of the sod-house frontier or the manners of vigilante Americans. But the main inspiration for our history (perhaps our ideology) is still the work of a frontier-historian who has an honored place in any account of popular culture: Frederick Jackson Turner.

A few years before the twentieth century began, at a meeting of professional historians in Chicago, the 32-year old Turner read a paper which contained what came to be called his "Thesis." The existence of free land, the son of Wisconsin argued, its continuous recession, and the advance of settlements westward explain American development. The true point of view for our history is not the Atlantic coast, but the Great West.

"The rapid and almost complete acceptance of Turnerian ideas," Robert E. Riegel notes, "soon produced a flood of references by historians, sociologists, novelists, playwrights, and in fact by almost anyone sufficiently literate to put pen to paper. The historic Turner essay seemed to rate only slightly lower in the popular estimation than the Bible, the Constitution, and the Declaration of Independence."[1]

To follow the extraordinary development of this thesis, and the resulting argument and revision it has produced, is not our purpose here.[2] From Daniel Boone to Spaceman, we have accepted the word "frontier" for any movement of exploration and adventure; any nationally urgent need; any program a Jefferson, Roosevelt, or Kennedy begins. When the virgin land ran out, the city, the Negro, automation, and the moon became "new frontiers." Coonskiners from the West are always ready to challenge Redcoats of the East, with the congealed idea of "frontier" to sustain them—rite words in rote order. This attitude certainly predates Turner; but he gave it classic formulation and historical respectability. Anyone who would revisit and reappraise regionalism returns to Turner as does the Moslem to Mecca.

What Turner sensed—and what the Sage of American regionalism documents—is the key role of mobility and motion in American life.

The "restless temper" that Alexis de Tocqueville encountered on our shores in the nineteenth century (Charles Dickens called it "instability") has dominated our history. We are planters without roots; settlers who can't settle down. As a poet (in this case, Edna St. Vincent Millay) put it:

> My heart is warm with the friends I make
> And better friends I'll not be knowing;
> But there isn't a train I wouldn't take
> No matter where it's going.

Turner saw America's epic journey in geographical as well as psychological terms. For him, the frontier was a "moving section"; a form of society determined by the interaction of man and land. The West was a "migration region"—a stage of society as well as a place. In order to conquer American history, he insisted on dividing it into eight distinct regions (New England, Middle States, Southeast, Southwest, Middle West, Great Plains, Mountain States, Pacific Coast), each with "its own special geographical qualities, its own resources and economic capacities, and its own rival interests, partly determined in the days when the geological foundations were laid down." Ours was no monolithic culture, but a land of potential nations, to be conquered and colonized, to rise through stages of development; each to interact regionally with the others, thus forming the United States.[3]

To this visionary, American history was an unfolding and a fulfillment. His chief contribution was not so much an hypothesis as a mystique. Inevitably his colleagues, some trained in hardheaded German factualism, challenged him. His monistic thesis was too simple for the complexities of American democracy and character. George W. Pierson suggested that Turner was either uninterested or incapable of rational anaylsis. Henry Nash Smith calls him a prisoner (though a willing one) of the agrarian tradition. Deriding the Turner Thesis (alias the Frontier Thesis, alias the Frontier Hypothesis) has become, for certain historians, a favorite indoor sport.

Often they miss the point: the frontier *has* become a congealed

idea, which urbanism, electronics, and circuitry have not melted.
Coonskinism *is* rampant in contemporary America. Even cigarette
ads yearn for Marlborough Country.

This can be observed on any day and any channel. America's
one unquestioned contribution to world mythology is the frontiers-
man. This romantic embodiment of freedom entered the Appalachi-
an forests as the buckskin clad warrior, to emerge on the Great
Plains a century later as the Cowboy. Somewhere between the
Alleghenies and the Rockies the sons of Daniel Boone traded coon-
skins for sombreros, long rifles for six-shooters, moccasins for boots.
During these same years a sports-ritual called baseball was developing.
Almost no changes in the rules for baseball and westerns have taken
place in half a century. They are frozen into dogma.

Many writers have delved into the history of the cowboy,[4] who
has ridden through whole libraries of dissertations, light novels, pulp
magazines and canned films. Rather than destroying him, television
merely gave him a new lease on life. The fascination is perennial. On
January 1, 1878 the Washington *Star* editor reported that "those
nomads of regions remote from the restraints of moral life" were
laws unto themselves. Cowboys "loiter sometimes for months, and
share the boughten dalliances of fallen women!" What red-blooded
American could be expected to turn his back on a cowboy story or
movie after *that*?

As Walter P. Webb points out, the cowboy novel furnishes a
peculiar difficulty for the author—he must write about a pastoral
and half-nomadic group for a body of settled and usually urban
readers who never see a cow until he is packaged in a supermarket.
That writers who have themselves never been west of Brooklyn suc-
ceed frequently in this difficult task seems to pique Professor Webb.
"If we could dispel the haze," he says in *The Great Plains*, "we could
view western life as it was in reality—logical, perfectly in accord ultimately with the laws laid down by the inscrutable Plains." We can't
dispel the romantic haze that has settled on the western horizon—
and we wouldn't want to, even if we could. That region of the nation
known as "the West" has not only mesmerized all neighboring regions,
but the whole wide world.

"As I sat in the movie house it was evident that Bill Hart was being loved by all there," Sherwood Anderson wrote in *A Story Teller's Tale*. "I also wanted to be loved—to be a little dreaded and feared too, perhaps. 'Ah, there goes Sherwood Anderson. Treat him with respect. He is a bad man when he is aroused. But treat him kindly and he will be as gentle with you as any cooing dove.' "

This is intrinsic regionalism. In the world's most mechanized culture, the Cattle Kingdom has changed beyond believing since the days of the old Chisholm Trail. In the extrinsic sense, cowboy lore is mere pageantry. But as a tangible safety valve for mechanized urbanized America—that's another thing. City-dwellers all over the land rush to the movie house or TV screen to see Westerns, which accommodate many kinds of meaning. Among these, John Cawelti has pointed out, are the archetypal pattern of heroic myth, the influence of media, and the need for social ritual. The successful formula has provided popular art and entertainment ever since Professor Turner's day.[5] Might not the cowboy be America's chief contribution to world mythology?

There are many other contributions, and popular stories, emerging from this soil. "Landscape" means many things to different people. On a hillside the poet might see intimations of immorality; the engineer, the place for a new sewer line. A farmer translates acres of land into so many bushels of wheat; a soldier into locations for cannon; an oil driller into potential well sites. The mind trains the eye. Landscape is the state of being derived from the inner mind of the inhabitants.

That is why young Americans, sick to death of the landscape we have made in Viet Nam, are so fascinated with American Indians, whose approach to land is basically religious. Their bold colors and stance allow them to confront our economic exploitation with stoicism or (as at Wounded Knee) with defiance. More and more Americans in the 1970's are coming to agree with John Collier's statement in the 1930's: "The Indians had what our world has lost. They have it now. What the world has lost, the world must have again, lest it die. Not many years are left to recapture the lost ingredient."

When the popular view becomes romantic, the daily reality

makes an automatic correction. Over this earth is a hot sun which scorches a hole in the popular imagination. Behind cuddly feminine names like Bertha, Dora, or Evelyn hide bone-breaking hurricanes. America is plagued by the continental waywardness of rampaging nature; by the cold blue wind in the day and the cold human blues in the night. From the beginning, in both our formal and popular history, our story has been one of painful separation and slow adjustment. Generation after generation the American earth has been both our greatest problem and blessing. We have not treated the earth well. Three of the nine inches of topsoil have been sacrificed; about nine tenths of the timber. The spiritual heir of Paul Bunyan is Tom Joad.

Slighted, gutted, glorified, littered, the American earth never has and never will lose its primacy. We cannot escape our landscape, nor build any estate removed from its reality.

Popular culture springs not from one but from two soils. The first is physical: from it comes materials which go inside our bodies, our machines, our warehouses, making our jokes, our electronic devices, and our books possible. The second soil is spiritual and feeds another part of us. From this soil springs the tradition, the archetypes, the formulae which cement us together. We live not only from the land, but from what love and laughter and feeling can make of those who work it. Here is the sinew of the soul, without which human meaning evaporates.

Two soils, two strengths. One strength is of the earth, the other of the human spirit. To study them separately and understand them jointly is the task of scholars.

4. HEROES

God, I'm glad I'm not me.

—Bob Dylan

Careful: there's cordite mixed with the popcorn.

—William Blissett

In the days of Eisenhower the Conqueror, the valleys stood so thick with corn that they laughed and sang. Content in one such Valley (of Virginia), I taught and wrote of American heroes. That was back in 1958 A.D. Ah yes, I remember it well.

Across the campus was the chapel in which my favorite hero, Robert E. Lee, lay buried. The Noble Knight, without blemish, without reproach; looking back to Washington's crusade to free the colonies, and forward to Eisenhower's crusade to free Europe. Lee had been nobly served by General Jackson (buried in the local cemetery), Eisenhower by General Marshall (trained at the local Virginia Military Institute). Everything fit, snug in the great Chain of Being— way back in 1958 A.D.

Exit Eisenhower, enter Kennedy. Suddenly everything was popping: empires, ideologies, arts, ghettoes, population, platitudes. Cold wars got hot, kids became cool, and God was said to be dead. Suddenly, a counter-culture, shouting its barbaric yawp from the roof-tops of Academia, was turning periods into question marks.

30

Ugly became beautiful, odd became normal. The key word was neither realistic nor romantic but psychadelic; not oral or verbal but multi-sensory; not improvised or planned but electronic. Pop went the hero.

Changes in American society since Eisenhower have been so profound, so rapid, that no one can fully evaluate, let alone measure, them. "What has happened," a Japanese observer notes, "is that substantial and structural problems have so shaken American society and politics that the institutions have lost their ability to restore themselves."[1] One corollary is that the heroes have lost their ability to inspire, the generals to lead. Arthur Schlesinger, Jr. wrote a much-quoted 1962 essay on "The Decline of Greatness." "Ours is an age without heroes. . . . We have no giants who play roles which one can imagine no one else playing in their stead."

Certainly there are few heroes modeled on those serenely confident Generals, elegant 18th century squires, bold 19th century industrial tycoons. The presidency itself suffered a sea-change under Kennedy: first president born in the 20th century, first from the political vortex of megalopolis, first Roman Catholic. The term "popular" took on a new meaning with the Kennedy Boys. So did "politics."

Out went purple prose and pious platitudes. His press conferences were masterpieces of relaxed, popular exposition. Here was the young aristocrat who was at home with new media, ideas, and life-styles.

Kennedy's assassination, in 1963, was the most crucial event in the heroic history of our generation. Because of the times and technology, Kennedy had a global popularity unlike that of any other president, or of any man then alive. That he should be killed senselessly by an ex-Marine, who was in turn killed on television before millions of viewers, formed an unbelievable historic episode—a happening.

This sense of the unexpected, the unbelievable, was flavored with a tang of the grotesque. As in a mixed-up movie, in which the film ran backwards, we found ourselves in 1964 watching Barry Goldwater campaigning for the presidency on horseback. Old timers who remembered Buffalo Bill were filled with nostalgia. Not so for most Americans. Even a Texas Ranger seemed better than this. Lyndon B. Johnson, the last of the 19th century presidents, took office.

The Johnson Years mirror the knotty and perennial American paradoxes: Virgin Land *vs.* Raped Landscape; Arcadia *vs.* Grub City; consensus *vs.* anarchy; citadel *vs.* caravan. Some sat in while others copped out. Consensus disappeared. A single catalytic agent, Viet Nam, changed oldstyle American military heroes into newstyle villians. Caught between the corncob and the computer, older Americans didn't know whether to go back to the farm or forward to the moon. Their children went to Woodstock.

There was no national mourning when a contemporary of John F. Kennedy—Woody Guthrie—died in 1967. Guthrie was a proto-popular hero who would be reincarnated in a talented imitator, Bob Dylan, and Woody's less talented son, Arlo. The ghost of Guthrie, as much as that of Kennedy, haunts the 1970's.

Left alone with his young brother in an Oklahoma shanty, Woody was an orphan of living parents. Most of his life was spent in compulsive, aimless rambling. Yet he left a body of work—over a thousand songs—which illuminate his whole period. "Some of them are purty dern left-handed," Guthrie admitted. "They are so left wing, I had to write 'em with my left hand and sing 'em with my left tonsil." Along with more learned contemporaries whom he never read or quoted—the Existentialists—Guthrie helped to put Anti-Hero on the center of the stage. So did Norman Mailer, who gradually emerged as the prototype author of his generation. Going through many changes after writing his best-selling novel about World War II (*The Naked and the Dead*), Mailer mirrored the cataclysmic changes that followed. His credo was clearly stated in *Advertisements for Myself*:

> The decision is to encourage the psychopath in
> oneself; to explore that domain of experience
> where security is boredom and therefore sick-
> ness; to exist in that enormous present which is

33

without past or future, memory or planned intention.

The heroic hobo was popular again. The word, thought to be derived from "Ho, boy," had been used for a century to describe homeless and penniless vagrants who first travelled the rails, then the roads. Strong backers of the Populist Revolt in the 1890's (did we re-stage the election of 1896 in 1972?), then of the Wobblies' labor movement, the hoboes have long sung their heady, anti-heroic songs:

> Hallelujah, I'm a bum!
> Hallelujah, bum again,
> Hallelujah! Bum a handout,
> Revive me again.

The new King of the Hobos was Jack Kerouac, whose best seller was called, appropriately enough, *On the Road.* This errant prodigal son from the Roman Catholic Church went on to write *Dharma Bums, Visions of Gerard,* and *The Subterraneans.* In his wake came the Hippies, city and politics-oriented, more anxious to do than to write. For them liberty, equality, and fraternity became turn on, tune in, and drop out. For thousands of Americans "finding myself" meant "freaking out." A whole new vocabulary of drug addiction cropped up. Often their protest was scattered and controllable: not at the 1968 Chicago Democratic Convention, or on the campus of Kent State in Ohio.

Historians stress that unheroic or anti-heroic characters are deeply rooted in the past—fool, clown, scapegoat, freak, rebel without a cause, angry young men. But never before have they been full-blown authentic popular American anti-heroes, pushing the oldstyle knights, generals, and moneymakers off the stage. At least so it seemed, on the surface; but were the old heroes destroyed or trans-formed? Were we not still entranced by what James Joyce calls in *Finnegan's Wake* a monomyth? Are our new popular idols—sometimes, like Nanki-Poo in *The Mikado,* disguised as second trombones

—brand new or retreads? Do they re-enact the old rites of passage: separation, initiation, return? Do they still venture forth from the world of common dullness to the region of fleeting wonder?

The heroic scene is changing too rapidly and we are too close to it to give final answers to long-range questions. We *can* say that changes in media, lifestyle, priorities, ideologies are reflected in our heroes. Motion pictures and television confer celebrity, for example —not just on people, but on acts, objects, places, ways of life. Everything is visible with the Big Eye; ethnic groups which were once under-viewed are now seen and discussed far out of proportion to their numerical strength in the total culture. Indians and Blacks wage large-scale campaigns against traditional American heroes. Writing of "The White Race and Its Heroes" in *Soul on Ice,* Eldridge Cleaver sees more need for shame than pride in our heroic past:

> That such venerated figures as George Washington and Thomas Jefferson owned hundreds of black slaves . . . and that every president since Lincoln connived politically and cynically with the issues affecting the human rights of most American people—these facts weigh heavily upon the hearts of the white youth.

His sneers at "Mr. & Mrs. Yesterday" have been repeated and echoed for a decade. Not only flesh-and-blood writers, but printer's-ink comic characters, have altered. Consider Superman. Created in the Depression as an icon, restlessly eager to embrace violent solutions, he has become alienated and disillusioned. Standing on top of a skyscraper, looking at ant-like humans below, he muses: "For the first time in many years I feel that I'm alone. . . ."

Even Superman isn't as alienated as a 1969 group chronicled in *Esquire.* Called the Chickenshits, they wore yellow armbands, carried a yellow flag, and played kazoos. When confronted by opposition, they dropped to the floor and crawled out mumbling, "Grovel, grovel, grovel, who are we to ask for power?" One notes that the anti-heroes or reluctant heroes remain strong in the 1970's.

Their admirers and chroniclers are proud to repeat what Craig Mc-Gregor, a devoted Dylanologist, says about Bob Dylan: "He is both anti-political and anti-intellectual. He is a Three-Minute-Twelve-track Super-acrylic-Longplay-Hero with an automatic cutoff at the song's end." Is that any way to run Olympus?

Why scrutinize and lionize Dylan? Because, the argument runs, he enacts the dilemmas and crises of the generation he represents. He has taken us through politics, drugs, transcendentalism, communes, love. . . . "What the hell else have we a right to ask of him?"

Or to ask of Janis Joplin (1943-1970), our Right-Here-and-Now Do-It-Baby who tried everything—including suicide? Suddenly famous for her work with a San Francisco group called Big Brother and the Holding Company, she was quoted as saying: "I don't know what happened. I just exploded." Don Heckman called her a study in tension—beads, fringe, and hair streaming in every direction, her hands constantly moving, like curiously delicate butterflies; drinking, cursing, crying, sometimes all at the same time. She was under thirty when she joined Jean Harlow, James Dean, Jackson Pollock, Jimi Hendrix, and Marilyn Monroe in the Cult of the Early Dead. "Janis designed her own package," her mother concluded, "and the package became the person."

Equally convincing as a barometer of the cultural scene is Joan Baez. On the surface she makes an unlikely cultural heroine. Born on Staten Island in 1941, a college drop-out and amateur guitarist, she was a surprise sensation at the Newport Folk Festival who tuned into politics with the 1963 "March on Washington." Anti-War and civil rights activities brought her fame and jail sentences; her husband was sentenced to three years in prison for refusing induction. Those who did not stand up for life in deed as well as in song, Joan said, were "irrelevant to the only real question of this century: how do we stop men from murdering each other?" Joan changed from a pacifist folksinger to a folksinger pacifist. She did not mind speaking out against things that displeased her—even Bob Dylan's songs, which she thought told young people that nothing matters, "I say the opposite," she said. "I believe everything matters, and you have to take a stand." In what other decade could a female pacifist have become a cultural hero? And what does her career tell us about changing patterns of American youth?

Women's Lib has been a major movement in our time—but it has not yet produced a national heroine. Many have echoed and reinforced Sarah Grimke's famous 1838 request: "I ask no favors for my sex—only that our bretheren take their foot from off our necks." But a new relationship between hero and heroine has not been widely understood or accepted. In a new book on *Cult Heroes of Our Time* (edited by Theodore L. Gross), Jacqueline Onassis is presented as "The Existential Heroine," a queen without court or clout, who was going to have her cake and eat it too.

For women and men, the heroic proposition is linked in to the new politics of visibility. We are dominated by images rather than words. Instant information cries out for instant solutions. Yet it does not follow that the heroic process is deteriorating, or the instinct for admiration and acclaim slipping. It may be that a generation which is better educated, more sophisticated, more travelled and media-exposed than any in history will demand and expect more from heroes. Because no highly publicized figure can any longer hide his contradictions, shortcomings, and recorded blunders, the old one-dimensional hero or paragon is finished. We have to accept the new crop warts and all, or not at all. Might this propagate the anti-hero?

Thus, one has to accept the contradictions inherent in a figure like Cassius Clay (alias: "The Lip" and "Gasseous Cassius") who changed his name to Mohammed Ali. Not only does he combine very different physical and spiritual attributes; he also moves beyond the role of boxer, to become poet, philosopher, critic. We see his disparities in life; for Marilyn Monroe, they emerged only in death. The stereotyped "dumb blonde" was actually a tragic figure; she knew and she cared very much. And what shall we say of the multiple roles of Bill Cosby, Jane Fonda, Joe Namath, Dick Gregory, or Richard Nixon?

Or the multiple sounds of Elvis Presley—the hero who popped in 1953, repopped in 1973, and became the most enduring and successful show business personality ever known? His 250 million records and 31 movies gave him an unmatched prominence. According to Gallup, his first name is better known today than any two names in the world.

And who can measure the long-range impact of the Beatles, four English youths born in the 1940's who became better known than the Four Disciples? After a nondescript beginning, including several group names (Moon Doggies, Silver Doggies, Silver Beatles) the "lads from Liverpool" became so famous that one of them, Paul McCartney, announced that they were better known than Jesus. Equipped with a private mythology and bizarre artifacts and clothes, they were made members of the Most Excellent Order of the British Empire—adopted by the very Establishment they had delighted in spoofing and mocking. The Beatles and their multiple followers produced their own style of music, dance, clothes, speech —and heroes. They were truly stylistic radicals, writing anthems for liberated youth. "The rock hero," Richard Goldstein has noted, "is a liberator in musicians drag. The remarkable thing about pop is that it can bring about rapport between a leader and his followers without ever resorting to dogma." How and why this comes about is only one of many new questions confronting students of heroes and hero-worship. We know far too little about the juxtaposition of public images and the impact of constant media-exposure on those who fascinate and inspire us. Only by responding to the public's insatiable passion for poetic stimulation can the hero remain "on top." No wonder frauds and deceptions are practiced and condoned. The crime may not be against people but against language. Or is it a "crime" at all?

Not only people, but whole movements move like meteors across the well-monitored skies. Not only Marilyn Monroe, but her once-idolized husbands, move quickly into contemporary archeology. "Where did you go, Joe DiMaggio?" And whatever happened to old Willie Loman?

He became *Fritz the Cat*—if not in Robert Crumb's underground reincarnation, at least in a slick X-rated full length Hollywood animated cartoon. From *The Greening of America* to *The Screwing of America* in half a decade. What about all those balding middle-aged middle class executives who ogle young ready-teddy secretaries and murmur, "I *am* Fritz the Cat?" How can we disentangle the heroic from the pathetic?

John Stickney tries to answer this question in *Streets, Actions, Alternatives, Raps: A Report on the Decline of the Counterculture.* Along the way he finds a young woman who sums up for him the treadmill which the counterculture set in motion: "I don't care where the form is, as long as we keep the motion going." But what happens when the merry-go-round breaks down?

Some at least still sing along with Crosby, Stills, Nash and Young:

> Rejoice, rejoice, we have no choice
>
> But to carry on!

To carry on is to change. In place of time-honored rural heroes (hunter, scout, cowboy) we have new popular urban heroes— detective, private eye, super spy. Like their earlier country cousins, they are all wanderers, diamonds in the rough, prepared for a violence they cannot escape. Girls play a much larger role than they did a generation ago. Your urban sophisticate is not a romantic lover, but he has good gonads; he is not seducing but seduced. This has produced a newstyle temple (i.e., cocktail lounge) prostitute, not so much interested in singing as in swinging.

The super spy is bonded, numbered, sent out on impossible missions. Like fantasy-heroes Mickey Mouse and Batman, he is immortal, irresistible, and international. Istanbul, East Berlin, and Hong Kong are all part of his traveling Disney World.

The prototype here is Ian Fleming's James Bond (007), who has been much imitated but never equalled. The private eye has a longer, more complicated lineage. He reminds us of Rex Stout's Nero Wolfe, Erle Stanley Gardner's Perry Mason, Dashiell Hammett's Continental Op. If he came white, he can be *Shafted* and blackened without damaging the formula or image. And he can slant his eyes a bit and become Dr. Fu Manchu (created by Sax Rohmer in 1913). Goods chasing and destroying bads will always be a breeding ground for popular heroes. The world of vicarious thrills and puzzles has endless variations and appeal.

In the days when super-stud Generals still were admired for all their stars, and men like MacArthur moved up and down river valleys, we sang this popular song: "Old Soldiers Never Die, They Just Fade Away." Well, they have faded—but other heroes have quickly lit up the sky with brightness and brashness. Pace and personnel have changed, but not the process. As Norman Mailer—writer, stud, film maker, popular hero—writes: "America is a country which has grown by the leap of one hero past another." That process is confusing and deceptive. Fact can blend with fancy, truth with fiction. That too is part of the territory. "Who cares what the fact was," asked Ralph Waldo Emerson, "when we have made a constellation of it to hang in heaven, an immortal sign?"

5. POP PRINCE

A prince once said of a hero slain, "Taller he seems in death."

—Ancient saga

John F. Kennedy's funeral was a landmark in American history. It demonstrated the power of electronic media to involve an entire population (indeed, much of the human race) in a vicarious ritual process. Whatever future historians decide about Kennedy as politician, strategist, administrator, we know this: his televised funeral raised him from passing president to Pop Prince.

"It was," David Bazelon wrote, "as if America had just discovered the fact of death—on television. What made death suddenly important was the unfulfillment of the dead man, which America recognized as its own unfulfillment."

Was the man or the media the message? Or were they so intertwined that the question is meaningless? We have clues from contemporary artists like Roy Lichtenstein: "Kennedy's lively, upstart quality and Pop-Heroic proportions are part of a legend."

Both John and Robert Kennedy are gone now, but indelible memories remain: unruly shocks of hair, touch football games, sailing ships, jokes with Jackie, Huck Finn smiles. John Kennedy was our first "mod" president, born in and molded by the new century; the first man in the presidency who refused to be "corny." Self-ridicule was a trademark. Like the best new writers, musicians,

40

comics, he flatted and deflated. "How did you become a war hero?" an admirer asked. "They sank my boat," Kennedy replied.

Or again: "Why did you give a cabinet position to your brother?" "I see nothing wrong with giving Robert some legal experience as Attorney General before he goes out to practice law." Robert practiced politics too. As his brother's alter ego and then as United States Senator, Robert reflected his brother's images and interests. His trips around the world strengthened his alliance with youth and rebellion. He always seemed much more at home with children than with adults.

When in the spring of 1968 Robert Kennedy became an announced presidential candidate, America wondered if another Pop Prince was to wear the crown. Not so. Only a few minutes after he acknowledged victory in the California primary Kennedy faced man's last and greatest enemy, death. An assassin's bullet entered his brain, and his career was ended. The spring of 1968 found both John and Robert Kennedy resting in graves overlooking the Potomac River, above the capital which they had seemed destined to rule.

What qualities made John Kennedy the Pop Prince? There were several. He seemed not only to accept change but to revel in it. New art and artists fascinated him; at the same time he abhorred sentimentality and triviality. Phoniness was not his bag but wit was. He used it not so much to destroy enemies as to disarm friends. He was the polar opposite of that admirable square, Dwight D. Eisenhower, who brought Kansas to Washington. Kennedy graced his era by accepting it.

He was not a self-made man, like his autocratic father, Joseph Kennedy. Bank president at 25, Joseph amassed a fortune, but raised his sons on skimpy allowances. This note (written in 1929, when John was 12) verifies the point:

> A Plea for a raise
> By Jack Kennedy
> Dedicated to my father,
> Mr. J. P. Kennedy

My recent allowance is 40 cents. This I used for
areoplanes and other playthings of my childhood
but now I am a scout and I put away my childish
things. . . . So I put in my plea for a raise of
thirty cents for me to buy scout things and pay
my own way more around.[1]

Educated at Brookline's Dexter School, Canterbury School, and
Choate, John graduated in 1935. Graduated from Harvard in 1940
cum laude in political science, he wrote a thesis which was published
as a book entitled *Why England Slept*. "If John Kennedy is characteristic of the younger generation," Henry R. Luce wrote in the
introduction, "many of us would be happy to have the destinies of
this Republic handed over to his generation at once."

By 1941 Kennedy was commissioned in the Navy, and in 1943
he had his first command—PT 109. On August 20 of that year the
New York *Times* carried a headline which, so far as I can discover, was
the first link of the name of young Kennedy with the word "hero":

KENNEDY'S SON IS HERO IN PACIFIC
AS DESTROYER SPLITS HIS PT BOAT

"He didn't make it any great hero story," his friend Torbert
Macdonald wrote. "Jack was an understater, but he also did make
the statement that at night, when you don't know what's in the water
beside you. . . . He didn't need to draw me a diagram. I knew how
he felt."[2]

Even in his 20's John Kennedy was on his way to being a hero.
The story after that is not only part of the public record, but of the
legend of our times; the bright young politician, the eligible bachelor,
the junior Senator from Massachussetts, the efficient organizer. His
tightly knit political staff (on which his brother Bobby, Ted Sorensen,
and Larry O'Brian held key spots) worked incessantly; in the summer
of 1960 at 43, he won a first-ballot Presidential nomination at the
Democratic National Convention.

In the ensuing campaign against Richard Nixon, it was the four national television debates held in September and October, that best revealed Kennedy's understanding of new media and opportunities. Cool and apparently nerveless, Kennedy showed an impressive command of facts and the ability to push Nixon into generalization. James Reston observed:

> Kennedy started like the underdog who wasn't supposed to be able to stay the course with the champ, but is winding up with more specific information on the tip of his tongue than Mr. Nixon, whose presentation was general and often emotional. Mr. Kennedy was curt and factual.[3]

On a cool media, Kennedy was ice, Nixon fire. One did not have to be Marshall McLuhan to predict which candidate benefitted most from the electronic encounter. Nor was it hard to guess why the Republicans broke off all negotiations for a fifth nationwide television debate. Experts estimated that 120,000,000 had seen at least one of the four debates. Nothing in the other 43 presidential campaigns had in any way approximated it. An opinion poll showed that 75% of those voters who had made up their minds on the basis of the debates had supported Kennedy. Pop goes the election.

So much has been written about the "Kennedy style" that no clear picture of just what it was, or how it functioned, has emerged. That he abhorred sentiment, purple prose, and trite comments, and yearned to bring art, poetry, and creativity into public places was apparent. His careful exploitation of mass media was a Kennedy hallmark; his press conferences were masterpieces of relaxed, confident exposition. Here was the old Roosevelt "Fireside Chat," made visible, with Prince Charming doing the chatting. Warm smile, quick jokes, dry wit, hands that stabbed the air: the style was the message.

"He has a mind quite unlike that of any other Democrat of this century," Richard Rovere wrote. "It is not literary, metaphysical and moral, as Adlai Stevenson's is. Whereas Mr. Stevenson's political views derive from a view of life that holds politics to be a mere fraction of existence, Kennedy's primary interest is politics."[4]

This point was developed further by Norman Mailer in his book called *The Presidential Papers*. Eisenhower had been the anti-hero, the regulator; his view was narrow, cautious, and planted in the life-logic of the small town. Kennedy was the new hero; dynamic, unsettling, accelerating to the psyche of the city. Mailer found in Kennedy "a suggestion of dry pen heat, his eyes large, the pupils grey, the white prominent, almost shocking, his most forceful feature: he had the eyes of a mountaineer."

With the coming of mass media and the Big Light, politics has also become America's favorite move, America's first soap opera, America's best-seller. To cope with these things, Kennedy developed a cool grace, almost an indifference. His manner was like the poise of a fine boxer—quick with his hands, neat in his timing, two feet away from his corner when the bell ended the round. Here was a new sense of proportion for a new America. Here in the midst of Pop Culture, was our Pop Prince.

"What is already evident is that the national pantheon has a new figure and a fine one," Gerald W. Johnson wrote. "It is, above all, the ideal of youth; when a nation has gained a symbol that can release the generous impulses of its young men and women it is fortunate beyond computation."[5]

In the era of instant replay, Kennedy's assassination, in November, 1963, took on the aspects of a Happening. The events quickly became part of popular mythology; the fact that the jigsaw couldn't be fitted together made the whole matter even more fascinating. The official Report of the Warren Commission increased, rather than ended, the controversy. Titles like *Who Killed Kennedy?* (Thomas G. Buchanan), *Unanswered Questions about President Kennedy's Assassination* (Cylvan Fox), *Rush to Judgment* (Mark Lane), *Were We Controlled?* (Lincoln Lawrence), and *Whitewash* (Harold Weisberg) reflect the mood of the times. By 1966 Thothnu Tastmona was able to compile a sizable book entitled *It Is As If: Curious Aspects Concerning the Manner of President Kennedy's Death*.

Not since Lincoln's assassination had there been such national trauma; and new electronic devices magnified it ten-fold. More important the whole style of their lives, and hence of their deaths, were different. Lincoln was folk; Kennedy was pop. The century between them had completely transformed the heroic style in America.

Lincoln's generation saw death on the battlefield, as the lucky few who saw his funeral train headed west recalled. Kennedy's generation saw death nightly on television; the central character of his assassination was the coffin, which transfixed the camera, just as the camera hypnotized us. Of course, later events turned us back to the living, and revelations about Kennedy blunders (especially at the Bay of Pigs and in Vietnam) made him seem less heroic to the new generation than he had to mine. His great political adversary had been Richard M. Nixon. Some might have thought from the 1972 presidential landslide that Nixon had become the generation's accepted hero-leader. Then came Watergate, the Agnew resignation, Cox firing, and gravest constitutional crisis of the century. Could it be that the president who had won the greatest electoral majority was the worst president in our history? Abraham Lincoln's popular comment proved true yet again: "You can't fool all the people all the time." John F. Kennedy began to seem like the admirable and honest leader of earlier reputation.

I believe that we shall have, when the century ends, these three major American heroes from our turbulent past: Washington the demigod, Lincoln the commoner, Kennedy the pop prince. They are the choices of the people—and will be the choices, I think, of history.

6. CELEBRITIES

He's the greatest!

—Anonymous
(becoming Unanimous)

She was incredibly beautiful. On the screen she exuded a tender warmth that made her unique and irresistable. When Jean Baker became a celebrity, ogled and admired by millions, she changed her name to Marilyn Monroe. In a few years she was, an embodiment, an institution, a doctrine, a fashion idol, a sex goddess. There wasn't anything or anyone she couldn't have. Then, at the peak of her career in her mid-thirties, she committed suicide.

Could it have been something else? Did Marilyn Monroe murder Norma Jean Baker?

Her tragedy was that she wanted to be recognized and understood as herself, not idolized as a celebrity—a thing to twang the male erotic nerve. She was so profoundly disturbed by the idea of not being accepted as a real person that she felt herself being destroyed and did nothing to resist that destruction. She was one of the tragic figures of our time.[1]

After her death she lives on to haunt us in the work of pop artists—symbol of the gorgeous, erotic, glossy embrace of cornflake materialism. This lost illegitimate child who killed herself with barbituates became a myth and died of it. She is a kind of monument to heroic obsolescence.

46

What she stood for was summed up in terms like "hot stuff," "some dish," and "a gorgeous piece." The key adjective for celebrities is *hot*—emotional, tactile, torrid. To end up with a girl like this is to be "hot stuff," and to "make the sparks fly." An earlier generation had praised the "Red Hot Mama's," who had "it." Mae West was a sex-celebrity for years, with her purring tag-line, "Why doncha come up and see me some time?" During World War II the life jacket which inflated when a sailor was in the water was known to the Navy as a "Mae West."

Her male counterpart was the incredibly hot (by now camp) hero, Rudolph Valentino. Dark and well-groomed, he breathed passion as he galloped over the hot desert playing such roles as *The Sheik*. Otherwise respectable ladies collected his cigarette butts and hid them in their bosoms. When he died suddenly, mass hysteria swept over many females. A cordon of policemen had to stop admirers from plucking off his buttons as his body lay in state.

But one who was hotter, and more celebrated than Valentino was already on the scene: Clark Gable, who was "leading man" not only on occasions to Mae West and Marilyn Monroe, but Mary Astor, Claudette Colbert, Greta Garbo, Ava Gardner, Greer Garson, Grace Kelly, Norma Shearer, Barbara Stanwyck, Lana Turner, and Loretta Young. Born in small-town Ohio in 1901, the big-eared youth quit school at 17 to become a day-laborer, than a bit actor known as Billy Gable. Married to a woman thirteen years his senior, who had been on Broadway and knew its ways, the dashing over-confident stage Clark Gable was "invented by his first wife." In 1924 he went to Hollywood, then to Broadway, then back to Hollywood. The special alchemy of the silver screen started to work. While Fairbanks was creating a celluloid Swashbuckler, Gable became the lover-adventurer, certain to get the girl and to come out way ahead. He was irresistible. Instead of asking for love he demanded it. This wholly authentic All-American Guy was by the mid-1930's a household image. "Who do you think you are?" a wisecrack of the times went, "Clark Gable?"

Blessed with rare strength and great endurance he reached his pinnacle as Rhett Butler in *Gone With the Wind*. (Thirty years later the revamped film is still breaking box-office records throughout the world.) At 59 Gable went to the Nevada desert to film his ninetieth picture, *The Misfits*. Marilyn Monroe was his leading lady. He was her fantasy-father as he went through the strenuous part. Shortly afterwards he died of a heart attack; four months after his death, Gable's only son was born to his fifth wife.

In the first half of the twentieth century the silver screen was plainly the best place for a "sex-queen" and a "he-man" to prosper. The movie camera confers celebrity not just on people but on objects and places. The camera brings stardom to everything it records —and thus breeds celebrities. That is why innovating film-makers like Ingmar Bergman, Michelangelo Antonioni, Francois Truffaut, Michael Cacoyannis, and Peter Watkins may be the Parson Weems' of tomorrow.[2]

Meanwhile the old print-oriented celebrity makes a last stand as Playboy. Like Mickey Mouse, he stands before the world in all his two dimensions—the creation of a living promotion story named Hugh M. Hefner.

Started in the mid-1950's on only $7,000, the first issue of *Playboy* Magazine wasn't dated, with the expectation that there might not be another. A decade later, with a circulation of 2.2 million, it was one of the nation's leading magazines. In its pages the Playboy model or stereotype is pounded into the reader: a sophisticated, urbane, affluent, promiscuous, mature bachelor. This goal, scholars have suggested is "what most Americans have long desired as a perfect style of life."[3]

The Lenin of the fast-spreading Sex Revolution, Hugh Hefner, tuned into the new hedonism and shrewdly turned it to his advantage. In addition to publishing he is involved with night clubs, concerts, a modeling agency, a television show, and assorted other ventures. From his half-million dollar home in Chicago, he directs his elaborate popstyle world, absolute master of over 700 "bunnies." His is the world of now, pop, hot. In his round bed, which revolves electronically, Hefner outstrips and updates all the boyhood dreams of an older generation; Tom Swift and his Sextronic Keyboard.

The real celebrity is not Hefner, but the *Playboy* rabbit.

(Similarly, Mickey Mouse, and not Mickey's creator, is the Message.)
The rabbit, ever-present symbol for Hefner, is always dressed in
expensive, fashionable clothes, off to enjoy such "in" activities as
yachting, skin diving, night clubbing, or racing foreign sports cars.
Sexy girls, scantily clad, are always near by, but they don't seem to
unnerve him. His eyes remain half-closed in a bored fashion; his
mouth turns up slightly at the corners, reflecting a smug self-satisfac-
tion. Here, at last, is a rabbit who is a man of the world. *Playboy*
is more than mere diversion and dream-fulfillment. Every issue
teaches readers the symbols, styles, and rituals of a real Playboy; the
attitudes, beliefs, and gestures that are required. The key is "cool
but active sophistication." A typical cartoon shows a husband duti-
fully serving his wife and her lover cocktails in bed.

To give substance to their reveries men buy keys for Playboy
Clubs in various American cities. While the magazine appeals largely
to a college-age audience, the Clubs serve an older clientele—men
who don't mind paying well to ogle "bunnies" who serve as waitresses
and hostesses. A lucky few can go right to Hefner's Chicago home
and watch bunnies swim nude in the great glass pool. In this world
clock and calendar are redundant. Night can be day, Tuesday can
be Saturday, if one has the cool and the courage to control his environment.

To be a celebrity, in Playboyland, one has to be multi-dimen-
sional; up on the latest authors and theories; equally at home at
diplomatic receptions and hippie beer bashes. The whole process is
full of wish-fulfillment and reinforcement. Here is a way to make
the scene, to be the talk of the town.

Celebrities are known for their well-knownness; notorious for
their notoriety. Such new-model "heroes" are nothing but ourselves
seen in a magnifying mirror. They are the perfect embodiment of
tautology: the most familiar is the most familiar.

Our generation has not only produced celebrities, but has recast
heroes in the new mold. Jesus becomes "no snob, but a regular
swinger," while God is (in James Thurber's satiric phrase) "my pal
Jehovah." Washington becomes an "everyday guy," and Lincoln
"just one of the boys." This tendency helps to explain the success

of a series of banal juvenile books called "The Childhood of Famous Americans" and the familiarity and vulgarity of current political campaigning.

In the spirit of the times, Earl Blackwell and Cleveland Amory compiled in 1959 a *Celebrity Register,* containing 2,200 biographies. "It is impossible to list accurately the success or value of man; but you *can* judge a man as a celebrity—all you have to do is weigh his press clippings." Thus do Bertrand Russell and Jane Russell move dos-a-dos down the pages of heroic history.

National culture is being replaced like the horse and buggy when the automobile came by a synthetic substance that exists in the media. "Entertainment" is never just entertaining, being chock-full of attitude-forming information. Ads not only sell—they shape. Not the illusion of progress, but the illusion of technique, ensnares us. Not our jobs but the texture of our personalities is endangered by the new lifestyle. The new American *imago* is couched not in terms of causes or events but of images picked up by our constant involvement in vicarious activities of the human race all over the world. In this sense our celebrities are exported, on film and paper, all over the world. They in turn are affected by, and are sensitive to, their global audience.[4]

New mass media (especially television) have greatly increased the visibility of the entertainer, and inflated his general importance. No movie star who has not been on TV rates as high with most Americans as even moderately successful TV stars. Publicists know that the best way to solve problems is to put entertainers on a pedestal that casts rational objects of respect and affection in the shade. The line between hero, artist, and salesman has merged.[5]

Nineteenth century Robber Barons grabbed natural resources and staged "The Great Barbecue." Now, in the twentieth century, we have show business Robber Barons who go beyond the old saw that business is business. Now show business is show business. By their celebrities ye shall know them.

These techniques affect politics, art, journalism, criticism, and education. Image-making is revealed in almost everything we do, say, or see. Television is chewing gum for the eyes. The question is no

longer "Do you like me?" but "Do you like my shadow?" Like the
people in Plato's allegorical cave, we mix illusion and reality, mistak-
ing the shadows for ourselves. We have turned from the three-dimen-
sional emancipator to the two-dimensional entertainer.

The boom in professional sports (especially football, basketball,
and hockey) has created scores of new celebrities. Playland is a car-
ousel world where movement, music, lights, and hysteria hypnotize.
Here is something Everyman can observe, interpret, and judge. He
can immerse himself emotionally and viscerally in sports and find
his identity there. They will play an increasingly important role in
popular culture and celebrity-making.

Not only players but sports themselves come and go—changes
in fads and styles are complicated. We know little at this time about
measuring the changing audience, the evolving aesthetic, the heroic
climate. What happened to the Beatniks and the Hippies? Just when
we decided that Rock Music was here to stay, the kids headed back
for the tunes of the '50's. Just when I learned to appreciate the
music of Jefferson Airplane it disappeared over the horizon.

The rule for celebrities is easy come, easy go. The new ones
bring a new sign and image—conjured up somehow out of the sub-
conscious. People under thirty usually accept the urban world forced
upon them—not the world which Daniel Boone pioneered or Henry
David Thoreau eulogized, but the world of neon light, billboards,
comic strips and strippers. The TV commercial is the new *lingua
franca*. The unreality of the environment is what makes it seem so
real.

Popstyle, from which celebrities emerge, makes of the phony
an epiphany. Shallowness, repetition, frustration are all built into
the model. "I find Andy Warhol's movies long and boring," the
playwright Edward Albee said recently. "But that's all right. I like
long and boring things."

My teen-age daughter is right. "Give your ulcer a break, Dad,"
she advises. "Don't fight it!"

7. ICONS

Man-made images are the American reality. What we
have is a fusion of the reality and the popular image of
it.

—Harold Rosenberg

The war of the icons has long been under way.

—Marshall McLuhan

Icons are images converted into plastic form. They stand for
or suggest something else. Icons have meanings as well as dimensions.
They are external expressions of internal convictions: "everyday
things" that make every day meaningful.

A Cadillac and a Volkswagon are both assemblages of steel,
glass, and rubber, but they are much more. People who sell, see, and
own them know this. They are icons. The very words "Cadillac"
and "Volkswagon" signify two different lifestyles. And what of the
Virgin Mary on the dashboard? An artifact, image, symbol, an icon—
plastic Catholicism for the Space Age! Thus do old and new icons
meet and blend on the turnpikes.

Pop icons are very new and at the same time very old. Of course
we do not admit to being traditional. But what Papal decree can take
St. Christophers' medals from sophisticated jet travellers? What college president dare order all amulets from around the necks of Black

Militants?

Icons accumulate and alter meanings; they also lose them. The iconic Virgin Mary does not speak to the twentieth century as she did to the thirteenth. The swastika does not motivate European youth of the 1970's as it did those of the 1940's. Man carries meanings, not merely objects invested with meanings. The image precedes the idea in the development of human consciousness; but the idea drives the image on to glory or oblivion.

In *Icon and Idea*, Herbert Read observes that "thinking in pictures" is the first stage of icon-making. The ensuing steps to the construction of icons were taken in the prehistoric period. All cultures invent icons. Freud spoke of "optical memory-residues—things as opposed to words." The mind is not so much a debating society as a picture gallery. We look with our eyes, see with our minds, make with our hands. Form and formula fuse. The word becomes flesh, and dwells among us.

The standard dictionary definition of icon (from the Greek root eikōn)—"an object of uncritical devotion"—does not penetrate layers of meaning and emotion which cluster around it. Icons are symbols and mindmarks. They tie in with myth, legend, values, idols, aspirations. Because of the great stress religion places on icons, some would limit icons to conventional religious images typically painted on a wooden panel.[1] I seek to revitalize the word and relate it to popular culture. Icons still move men, even when they are not recognized as such in supermarkets, discotheques, used car lots, and funeral parlors. They pop up on billboards, TV commercials, and magazine covers. Manna may still come from heaven; but much daily information flows through the Big Tube, which constantly flashes images and cools outer reality.

Icons traditionally connote fixity and permanence; but pop icons deal with the flux and impermanence of contemporary Protean Man. A style of self-process and simultaneity is emerging; icons, like everything else, adapt accordingly. Objects are the building-blocks; ideas the cement holding them together. Modern man is starved for ideas and objects that give coherence to electric-age culture. What he finds most acceptable, Robert Jay Lifton notes, are "images of a more fragmentary nature than those of past ideologies. These images, though often limited and fleeting, have great influence upon his psychological life."[2]

With all the changes icons are still omnipresent. The old process continues: history becomes mythology, mythology begets ritual, ritual demands icons. Concepts end up as creeds and icons. Careers of men as different as Buddha, Christ, Marx, Einstein, and McLuhan confirm it. In secular times religious icons remain.

Millions live without much pain in a world where God is dead. But we can't exist long without images. Living in the Secular City, we crave and create a new physical and phychic environment. In our time the icon goes pop.[3]

The tombs of ancient Egypt were full of icons. There is a long unbroken history of sacred manna-bearing objects throughout history. Christianity continued the use of iconography. "I have seen a great many portraits of the Saviour, of Peter and of Paul, which have been preserved up to our times, "wrote Eusebius, Bishop of Caesarea in Cappadocia (265-340). The catacombs were icon centers, used by simple people as well as the ecclesiastical hierarchy. The meaning and language of icons was a major strength of Christendom for centuries. Old and New Testaments yielded up scores of symbols, themes, and inspirations; with every new saint new iconographic possibilities emerged. Key words were legend, belief, sacred object, veneration. Then and now icons are associated with age and class groups. They demand a cult, a lore, a spot of veneration. "All sacred things must have their place," Claude Levi-Strauss notes. "Being in their place is what makes them sacred. If taken out of their place, even in thought, the entire order of the universe would be destroyed."[4] What is central to the concept of icon is touching a center near man's essence. The content is the criterion of form.

By 1970 we have reached "Post Time"—post-modern, post-Freudian, post-Marxian, post-humanist: but not post-icon. Today, as in every epoch, men want to make sense out of the universe, in the context of time, place, belief. Even "natural" facts of birth, growth, and death are reacted to in a "cultural" fashion.[5] The style that develops is *sui generis*, of its own order. Former styles lasted for generations, even centuries; but in a single generation we have radically altered ours. The consequences are profound and traumatic.

Help wanted: pop iconologist. Instead of indiscriminate praise or damnation of popstyle (two current postures) why not devise new criteria and categories for intrinsic meanings? Profiting from Erwin Panofsky's *Studies in Iconology* (1938), we should apply the same serious analysis to the current American Renaissance as was used for the older Italian and French. This would involve not only surface data (identification, description, authentication) but interior qualities (evaluation, interpretation, significance). It would also require an openness to popular culture which is notably absent in most parts of the academic community.

A hundred years ago Baudelaire invited fugitives from the world of memory to come aboard to seek the new. Subsequently there developed what Harold Rosenberg calls *The Tradition of the New* (1959). There have been few scholarly studies of it; few efforts to document Op, Cool, Retinal, Hard Edge, Post-Painterly Abstraction, LeNouvelle Tendence, Programmatic, and Psychedelic phases of painting, and simultaneous developments in other arts. Nor have the other items covered in this book received adequate attention. The quality of feeling is intense but incoherent—like being thrust into Kubla Khan's electronic pleasure dome.

Iconologists must seek a point of significant beginning. This involves not only comparative study between arts, but configurational analysis of the total *gestalt*. Scholarship and criticism must catch up with performance. If today's poets and artists are (as they have always been) joint bearers of a central pattern of sensibility, let's find out what that pattern is. American Studies: begin here.

The mainstream of iconology in our time—because of its dissemination through mass media—is the popular stratum of our culture. The mechanized trivialized standardized world of which elitists complain provides the raw material for a new lifestyle. That pop artists have singled out objects for extensive use is an iconic clue. Ever since Robert Rauschenberg's 1958 "Coca-Cola Plan" that famous container, which Craig Gilborn calls "the most widely recognized commercial product in the world," has been featured.

The history of soup cans was altered by Andy Warhol; no hamburger will ever be the same after Claes Oldenburg's pop depiction.

Coke bottles and soup cans are apt motifs not because they are unique but because they are omnipresent. This means that in the old traditional sense they are anti-icons. Note how the nature of icons has changed between the Age of Faith and the Age of Atoms. The Coca Cola company jealously protects its trade mark and 1915 bottle design while putting those marks and bottles in every hamlet of the world. Pop icons are not only accessible; they are unavoidable.

Does it offend you to think that a TV tube, a Coke bottle, and a soup can feature in pop iconography? Are they not building blocks of the new Secular Culture? The Greeks had their Olympus; the Romans their triumphal arches; the Christians their shrines. Once these were all new—and "pop." Newness implies obsolescence of form and value; icons fade even as we venerate them.[6] Another name for the Holy Grail is New Style or New System. Putting the adjective "new" in front of a noun doesn't cancel connections with the old. The search for the new may indeed exalt the old. Camp Style of the 1960's suddenly put Victoria back on the throne, while the film hierarchy was making room for two-bit Depression day gangsters Bonnie and Clyde. Critics like C. Ray Smith now exalt "the bold new poly-expanded mega-decoration" as we enter the Age of the Nude Light Bulb. Simultaneously, a reprint of the 1897 Sears Roebuck catalog became a national best-seller. What were Americans looking for in those pages of outmoded icons? What did they find?

We see not only with our eyes but with the camera which has become Everyman's Third Eye. Is the camera itself an icon of our age? Perhaps not, since as an instrument it *transmits* rather than symbolizes images. Not even photographers keep old cameras. The camera reaches its symbolic peak swinging from the necks of tourists around the world. But then it is an amulet rather than an icon—a charm which gives the wearer magic power.[7]

But surely the canvas or assemblage featuring the coke bottle, as well as the bottle itself, is an icon: an image converted into plastic form. Ideas like mass production, distribution, and taste become real in the three dimensional coke bottle (or canvas on which it appears). Only in music has the validity of popstyle won wider recognition than in art. Pop icons have been both identified and enshrined (if we can borrow that sacred word for our secular culture) by artists like Andy Warhol, Robert Rauschenberg, George Segal, Robert Indiana, Claes Oldenburg, and Roy Lichtenstein. Theirs is not the world of forests and wheat fields, but of automobiles, comic strips, junk yards, and go-go girls. The whole apparatus of retail emotions, gadgetry, and packaging is material for their art. They exalt the thingness of things.[8]

"I am for art you can sit on," Claes Oldenburg writes. "I am for the art of fat truck-tires and black eyes. I am for *7-Up Art,* Pepsi Art, Sunkist Art . . . the art of tambourines and plastic phonographs and abandoned boxes tied like pharaohs."[9] His subject matter is pop iconography. His objects (or icons) are commonplace, but his underlying theory is startling. Neither Oldenburg nor any of his contemporaries has put it as succinctly as Walt Whitman: "A mouse is miracle enough to startle sextillions of infidels."

In the Middle Ages, all experience found visual form in a single metaphorical system. Will we live to see this same phenomenon occur in the 20th century?

8. ART

The things I want to show are mechanical. Machines
have less problems.

—Andy Warhol

The 19th century is gone forever; but the words of Victorian
poets still haunt us—like these, by Rudyard Kipling:

And the first rude sketch that the world
    has seen was joy to his mighty heart,
Till the Devil whispered behind the
    leaves. It's pretty, but is it art?

The fiendish question still applies in a world filled with op, pop,
and bop. What about Yves Klein, sitting in a white room, *thinking*
pictures, some of which were sold? Or peelable sculpture, which
eventually leaves the owner nothing? Or "Drawing by Willem de
Kooning, erased by Robert Rauschenberg"? Intriguing—but is it art?
Grope for a definition. Art is, among other things, the will to
"form; intuitive apprehension; sublimation; the self-objectification
of feeling; an escape from chaos; pattern informed by sensibility;
distortion; liberation of personality; man speaking to men; an act of
love toward humanity; the direct measure of spiritual vision."
For every definition there's a counter-definition: words, words,
words. Never mind, we say, hiding behind the shield of St. John.

58

"In the beginning was the word." Recent linguistic research denies it. In the beginning was the *thing*. When the object (be it flesh or not-flesh) needed and got a name, then came the word. Are you *sure*, the anthropologist asks. Pushing back beyond the thing, does one not find that in the beginning was the *function*. All certainty vanishes; the argument rages on.

This much seems certain: nothing *begins* as art. Objects come into being as *something* to be measured on the scale of desirability. The "something" may be a chair, arrowhead, painting, or palace. Producing them, rather than the abstraction "art," is primary. Think of a line, one end of which is form and the other function. On that line man-made things are placed and judged. Some receive the label "art."

In all societies the artistic (or esthetic) impulse expresses itself according to traditional needs and standards. The channel through which individual effort flows is sanctioned form. Some variation is admired; too much is rejected or outlawed. Thus art, like every human activity, is a captive of the culture in which it originates. Art springs from man the maker: tool-maker, image-maker, myth-maker, homemaker, system-maker, city-maker, nation-maker. The line separating art from non-art is always conjectural; the wall dividing art from artifact is arbitrary. In any cultural court of judgment, Consensus and Circumstance reign as king and queen.

For example, consider the determination of "value." Isn't Mozart's music priceless? Apparently not to his contemporaries, who all but let him starve to death. And do you remember the sign in the German opera house: "This way out in case of Wagner"? Wouldn't anyone prefer a sparkling diamond to a rusty nail? Not the man trying to shoe his horse.

This is not to say that there is no pattern or hierarchy in the realm of creativity. Frequently a succession of different forms—in paintings, buildings, linguistic structures, social systems—are explainable by an inner logic, the passage from an antecedent to a subsequent stage. Vasari showed it in his survey of painting techniques, Bannister Fletcher in the evolution of architectural styles, the Grimm brothers in tracing linguistic changes. Sir James Frazer noted remarkably similar apples growing on his golden bough; Joseph Campbell's hero found old heroes reappearing with new faces. Can we, by extending the inner logic that guided them, answer the Devil's question once and for all?

Perhaps; but inner logic is hard to discern. There seem to be two major barriers; inner semantic confusion and outer insistence on categories. Far too often we seem quite literally not to know what we're talking about. Even when we can read words, we are unable to "read" the objects to which they point and refer.

Stylistic terms (classic, romantic, baroque, rococo, modern) are subjective and evasive, yet we treat them as if they were geographical certitudes. Or else we lump several together—English Gothic, French Baroque, and Chinoiserie, for example—and say it results in Chippendale. Others prefer dynastic labels—Ming vase, Louis XIV chair, Georgian architecture. But which George? If your informant means George III (who ruled for sixty years) is it early, middle, or late Georgian? And what about the popular label "William and Mary," tacked onto things that flourished long after their reign ended? Dare we admit that the terms and labels used so frequently are only, at best, averaged-out nominative generalizations?

Words by their very nature tend to reduce everything to the linear and the successive, just as computers reduce everything to a series of either-ors. They only approximate truth. Rather than serving as a liberating hero, Johann Gutenberg and his movable type may have opened the door to a world that takes us away from whole and valid experience into falsehood, rationalism, and fragmentation, as Marshall McLuhan argues in *The Gutenberg Galaxy*.

Not in words, but in things and actions, is essential meaning buried. Walt Whitman went on to ask those who would "talk or sing of America" if they were "faithful to things":

> Do you teach what the
>   land and sea,
> the bodies of men, womanhood,
> amativeness, heroic angers teach?

The answer is no. We verbalize. No one is *against* verbalizing. But can we not be taught to use our hands as well as our vocal cords? To suggest it brings anguished cries from some intellectuals. Handicrafts are for Boy Scouts, vocational schools, old ladies. To be significant, they insist, one must either speak or scribble.

But are not non-scribblers vital in building and maintaining civilization? Will any mere peroration repair a broken axle, set a broken arm, rectify a broken treaty? Is the word divorced from flesh meaningful? Isn't American culture expressed in the Brooklyn Bridge as much as in Hart Crane's poem about it? (A splendid structure, the Devil volunteers—but is it art?)

The imbalance that dominates modern art reflects and accentuates the imbalance written into the premises of modern educational theory. With considerable careful instruction, students can be taught to read Hart Crane's poetry. But who teaches them to "read" Brooklyn Bridge—or any other cultural artifact—not as factual syllogisms but essential truth? "Reading" objects is not a single problem but a whole cluster of them. To begin with, one needs to know how art historians deal with style, form, and intrinsic value; how anthropologists handle role, function, and diffusion. In addition to identification, description, and authentication, the more subtle matters of evaluation, interpretation, and significance must be dealt with. What angle of vision should the "object reader" assume? Or can he switch perspectives as he goes along?

"I am collecting the history of our people as written into things their hands made and used," Henry Ford stated in 1940. "A piece of machinery or anything that is made is like a book, if you can read it." A generation later, his *if* remains a stumbling block. Where objects are concerned, we still lack techniques of internal criticism, such as those scribblers have developed, to extract meaning from mute objects. The manuscript *tells* us what the writer meant to say. But what does the bronze head or stone face tell us? Precisely nothing. Instead of considering artifacts as cracks in the door of history we tend to dismiss them as relics.

Such a posture is disastrous because it puts vast amounts of material and data off bounds. In the United States, the mainstream in pre-Civil War arts (both for the Indian and the white man) was in the hands of the craftsmen. Art in a rural democracy neither has nor seeks the aristocratic trappings and status of the old monarchies. Nor does it tremble before abstract theories. Throughout its history, our nation has been more dedicated to Aristotelian things than to Platonic thoughts. Our Founding Fathers planted wheat, tobacco, and cotton as well as colonies. Thomas Jefferson had a flair for ideas--but he was a tinkerer and inventor, too. Realism and authenticity in politics, literature, or business, have prevailed. (Think of Jackson and Lincoln, Twain and Hemingway, Edison and Ford.) It is true that the immigrants looked for a Garden of Eden—but on the Great Plains they fenced it with barbed wire.

Another kind of barbed wire has kept the "fine" arts away from the majority of Americans. In the early years of this century, socially ambitious people "captured" the arts and class-typed the galleries and museums. Painting, sculpture, and the decorative arts were controlled by coteries. Like polo, debutante balls, and yachting, art was considered by many to be a landmark in Gentleman's Country. College and university art departments catered to those who would later become patrons, and resisted efforts to integrate their material in a liberal arts education. "Precious" and "effete" were adjectives applied to the "arty" set. As late as 1950, enrollment figures in art courses and departments were shockingly low; many of the best ones were in affluent girls' schools. After all, upperclass females would later "run" the art world, perpetuating the social attitudes they had inherited.

Most museums and galleries accepted this phenomenon and went along with the exclusionist point of view. In the generation before World War II, America's art museums (with some exceptions) were muffled and subdued. Guards chatted with visitors to break their lonely vigils. Art in America was a hothouse plant.

Suddenly all this changed. One major factor was the exodus of many European artists (Mondrian, Léger, Chagall, Ernst, Zadkine, Masson, and Breton among them) to the United States. World cataclysm altered all aspects of life. Art, like the atomic bomb, exploded. The fallout went everywhere. No one was sure of his status–artist, collector, curator, critic–but everyone wanted to be "in" on the next development. With unprecedented vitality, art zoomed off in a dozen different directions, featuring the primitive, abstract, three dimensional, calligraphic, or surrealistic. Symbolic acts took on visual forms. Here was an apocalyptic vision of a civilization gripped in revolution and terror, a raw display of authentic intensity. The Devil's question was irrelevant.

A single figure symbolized the new break-through–Jackson Pollock (1912-56). Tall, rugged, and partially bald, he gave the impression that every word he spoke cost him something of his life. Covering huge canvases with glowing bands of color, Pollock's tangles of lines and spots emerged in jungle-like patterns. With the "splatter-painters" form and color were not to be thought of as static spots, but as living energies in space. The artist's job was to release that living energy and thus electrify the viewer.

"Every so often a painter has to destroy painting" wrote a leading artist, Willem de Kooning. "Cézanne did it. Picasso did it. Then Pollock did it. He busted our ideas of a picture all to hell. Then there could be paintings again."

With daring and strength men like Pollock, de Kooning, Tobey, Rothko, Smith, and Kline filled their work with the drama, anger, pain, and confusion of contemporary life. A large-scale reaction against the "good taste" and shallow eclecticism of pre-war America got underway; the snobby old standards became the whipping boys of new tastemakers. They did indeed "knock the hell" out of old ideas about art.

There was a positive note, too–the plea for new methods of interpretation, such as those that scientists and diplomats had salvaged from the upheaval. Art had moved from realism to reality, mirroring an infinity of profiles. Following Paul Klee, artists devised a calligraphy free from representational service, abounding in fleecy line-flickers and instantaneous joy. Here was a summing up of the invisible to the realm of the visible.

Let the Devil scream (as indeed he and numerous now out-moded critics and dealers did) that this could never produce "finished works of art." The restless ricochets of line and color reflected the plight of man, harassed by today's problems and undone by visions of tomorrow's. The flowing patterns and irrational explosions marked art deliberately at war with a rational, mechanistic civilization. Frightened by what they saw, some labeled it inhuman. Others saw the new art function as the ancient cement that binds human communities together.

New York became the new art capital of the world. The child had become father of the man.

In the 1950's a new esthetic theory began to emerge, to accommodate what had in fact happened. Marcel Duchamp, a displaced European who had himself been art's *énfant terrible* a generation earlier, suggested that it be called the esthetics of impermanence. In today's world an art object is merely an interlude; an interval in the life of the maker or viewer; a temporary energy center, which glows like a light bulb for a certain time, then goes out. The play, symphony, or painting retires, leaving its imprint or image in a catalogue or monograph. Such impermanence is both a cultural fact and a stylistic device. His famous nude, Duchamp was quick to admit, has descended the staircase for the last time. In 1913 she was a cause célèbre. In 1974 she is dead.

Artists, as well as their works, come and go with terrifying rapidity. Jackson Pollock was killed in a sports car accident, leaving a dozen lesser figures to fight for the supremacy he had held. The critic Allen Kaprow assessed his impact in the October 1958 *Art News*:

> Pollock left us at the point where we must become preoccupied with and even dazzled by the suggestion, through paint, of our other senses, we shall utilize the specific substances of sight, sound, movement, people, odors, touch. . . . Out of nothing we will devise the extraordinary. People will be delighted or horrified, critics will be confused or amused, but there will be the alchemies of the 1960's.

Now, in the 1970's we know this was true. The alchemies

worked, and American art—multi-level and multi-faceted—has won its first world audience and following. Thus it has become both a part of, and a catylist for, the new international style.

9. BACK COUNTRY

I dreamt I was there, in Hillbilly Heaven. . . .

—Tex Ritter

Country, western, country-western, mountain, old time, familiar, dixie, gospel, cowboy, hillbilly, hill and range, western swing, Nashville, bluegrass, rockabilly. This is where the popcorn grows. Don't sneer. Not only that corn, but the bushel baskets of the money it earns, is green.

Behold Back Country American: uneducated, unsophisticated, unrepentant; self-righteous, religious, unilinear.

Stunning paradoxes: the virgin land—and the raped landscape. Arcadia—and Grub City. The Big Sky—and the Skyscraper. The American dream—and the American nightmare. Soul—and sadism. Caught between the corncob and the computer, do the old cliches help?

There is no acceptable etymology of the word "hillbilly." As early as 1505 the Scots used "billie" as a synonym for fellow or companion; the word hillbilly appeared in print only after 1900 and only as an Americanism. In recent years it is found linked with nouns like *music, song, ballad, show,* or *record.*

Abel Green was the first American writer to combine *hillbilly* and music in print, in the December 29th, 1926 issue of *Variety* magazine. "Hillbilly" was catchy (like jazz, swing, pop). Elasticity to meet new needs and media. It was another word in a long and

66

colorful list describing rural Americans: *poor white, lubber, cracker, peckerwood, tarhill, woolhat, cajun, redneck, sandhiller, appleknocker, ridge-runner, swamprat, claveater,* and *turdkicker.* Long before the term "hillbilly" was current the stereotype was widespread not only in America but Europe.

Feuding, hunting, and commanding were prerogatives. There was an Old Testament flavor to this land beyond the law. The operating word was *patriarchal.* A raw, Darwinian environment favored those strong of limb and will. Spinning wheels, banjos, weaving looms, and dulcimers flourished. So did authentic folk culture that would feed both fakelore and poplore after World War I.

In 1925 the "Grand Ole Opry," a weekly program of country music fresh from the corn fields, made its debut on Nashville's radio station WSM. Forty years later it was the oldest continuous show on radio, although country music was by then a large force on television too. Nashville boasted over 20 recording studios and innumerable talent agencies, record-pressing plants, music publishing houses, record companies and songwriters. Names like Chet Atkins, Bobby Goldsboro, Johnny Cash, Jeannie Riley, Tammy Wynette, Glen Campbell, Roger Miller, Tex Ritter, Roy Acuff, and Pat Boone had won not only national but international standing. England's "Country Music" spot on the B.B.C. was drawing five million listeners. Japan had worked out a Grand Ole Opry of its own; children who spoke hardly a word of English picked up lyrics about mountain dew, fried chicken, and corn pone. The iron curtain melted before the onslaughts of banjo pickers using the "Nashville Sound," created by Chet Atkins as artist and repertory man for Victor Records for almost a generation.

What made this music so popular all over the world? Why did it seem so "typically American" to non-Americans?

If the recordings and the recorders flourished, the hillbilly himself withered as a new industrialized America emerged on the postwar scene. History left him standing on his mountain peak, an outmoded rifle and ideology his only possessions. Unable to adapt he became ridiculous. Once feared and respected the hillbilly became the Pathetic Patriarch.

The change was heralded by a popular new stereotype in the American theater. He has disappeared now but Toby was the darling of tent repertory companies and small town theaters for three decades. Though scholars find proto-Tobies in characters like Sample Switchess and Tom Twinkes, it was Tobe Haxton, created in W. C. Herman's 1909 melodrama *Clouds and Sunshine* that set the style for a whole generation.

Audiences loved the "darn fool Toby." Fred Wilson's success in the part was accidental. "I came into this world with a shock of unruly red hair and a flock of freckles," he wrote. "Toby was myself plus a hickory shirt, patched jeans, boots with run-down heels, and a battered hat." Here was the hillbilly as buffoon. Uncouth and un-cultivated, he was a parody of the frontier which was suddenly as out-of-date as the horse and buggy.

As Albert F. McLean points out in *American-Vaudeville as Ritual,* Toby emerged during a period of crises in American social life. Modernism was changing everything. City life and proto-pop were becoming the new norm. Progressive people were determined to leave the hills behind. Seeing what a silly bumpkin Toby was merely reaffirmed this determination. If the big city seemed wicked to small town citizens, all the more reason to yearn for it. Fred Wilson played Toby as a believable character; those who followed played him essentially for the low comedy element, the grotesque clown.

In the novels of Erskine Caldwell, the clown crawled around on all fours. *The Bastard* and *Poor Fool* were followed by *Tobacco Road* (1932). The "hero" is Jeter Lester, a deceitful, lascivious fellow who reduces everything around him to animality. As a Broadway play *Tobacco Road* broke all box office records. In the 1940's people went to see it for the same reason that our children flock to super-spy stories; sex and violence never go out of style. The post-World War II hillbilly world, in cartoons, films, and plays is a world of Gothic horrors, in which latrines, looting, and lovin' prevail. These are the *folk*. The stereotypes are often *fake*. They provide vivid material for *pop*.

How easy to parody and ridicule *this* America; we are not many steps away from the T.V. Beverly Hillbillies. Yet even this television spoof has roots in sociological reality. Elmore M. Matthews' *Neighbor and Kin: Life in a Tennessee Ridge Community* (1966) documents the native distrust of education and special skill and the need for scapegoats. In the Atomic Age moonshiners still protect stills by telling stories of haunted stumps, creaking rocking chairs, phantoms, and ghosts that devour all who walk after dark.

The man country music champions has the "unhappies." Like the cowboy, another anachronism, he is landlocked and lonely. While the cowboy refuses to become involved with women (being faithful instead to his horse), the hillbilly proves the folly of involvement. Invariably he is cuckolded. Ma's good, Pa's lazy, the wife cheats. Call it corn if you will but it fills and sustains millions of people. There has always been plenty of corn in the popular American diet.

All of which raises the question: why does the Back Country remain so important in a rapidly urbanizing, technological society? Why do we fight our way through the tense city traffic to relax in front of the tube and watch the hayseeds cavort in "Hee Haw"?

Because, with all our sophistication and electrification we are still close to the earth. Scholars say that folk culture and popular culture are different; but most people never worry about that difference.

It is part of contemporary folklore to say that folk culture and the Back Country is finished. But this vast body of knowledge, handed on by tradition—by mouth, practice, custom—is still very much with us. Folklore is first cousin to mythology. Patterned on common experience, it is indigenous and indelible, and keeps cropping up in our popular culture.

That is why our young, strumming their electric guitars, yearn for attachments their industrial urban environment has denied them. In ghetto basements they dream of pink cherry blossoms and a sow that got the measles and died in the spring. Amidst the sirens' screeches they reaffirm that "never did hoof of beast go down on a lark's nest." The Ecology Crusade is another manifestation of our folk longings. One of the Old Boys who keeps making it with the young is Henry David Thoreau.

Thoreau was making it at Walden when the word "folklore" was coined by William Thomas. (The fact that the very word was devised to encompass *popular* material is significant.) The Folk-Lore Society of England was founded in 1878, the American Folk-lore Society in 1888. Ever since the struggle to define "folklore" has raged. The *Dictionary of Folklore, Mythology, and Legend* gives 21 definitions, in which five words are key: oral, transmission, tradition, survival, and communal. Behind all these and many other definitions one paramount truth remains. Woodrow Wilson put it this way: "The vitality of life does not come from the top to the bottom, but like a great tree, from the soil up."

The American tree has roots that go back into the soil of Africa, Europe, and even Asia. We shall say something about the black heritage in another chapter; meanwhile, a glance at Europe.

The connection between European folklore and American variations is well documented and convincing. One of the best known examples is "Barbara Allen," a ballad that crossed oceans and mountains with ease. The essential tale is that of a young girl who scorns her lover, Sweet William (or Willie, Sweet Jimmy, Young Johnny, or Jimmy Grove). Pepys praised a rendition by the celebrated London actress, Mrs. Knipp, in 1666. He would have been surprised to know that generations later Americans were singing:

> Way down South where I came from
> Is where I got my learning.
> I fell in love with a pretty little girl
> And her name is Barbey Ellen.

"The Two Sisters" became "Sister Kate" in the New World. This time a jealous girl pushes her younger sister into a mill stream for stealing her suitor. The European version has the miller, who recovers the body, performs magic on various parts of the corpse; in America this aspect was dropped, and the story became a children's game. Magic was transformed into merriment and folklore prevailed.

In "The Gypsy Laddie," a fair lady gives herself to a roving gypsy. Her lord returns, finds her gone, chases after and rescues her,

and hangs fifteen of the gypsies. In adaptations which have come
to light in Virginia the retribution and hanging are omitted. Instead,
the lady decides to cast her lot with the roaming vagabonds—a
decision that might well have appealed to the hard-pressed trail-
blazers moving into frontier territory:

> How can you forsake your house and land
> How can you forsake your money O?
> How can you forsake your sweet little babe
> To go with the gypsy laddie O?
>
> O, I can forsake my house and lands
> O, I can forsake my money O,
> O, I can forsake my sweet little babe
> To go with the gypsy laddie O.
>
> She was used to a feather bed
> And servants all around her,
> And now she has come to a bed of hay
> With gypsies all around.

"The Three Ravens" was revamped on this side of Atlantic into "The Three Crows." Back in the Appalachians you might still
hear the macabre song which moves forward with such elemental
power. But these Anglo-American ballads didn't merge into a common folklore, even when members of various folk elements merged
into a larger recognizable American culture. The cement binding
America together isn't traditional folklore but images and techniques
of the popular media.

Local legends, tied to the landscape in which they arose, do
flourish. But such legends, transmitted to outsiders, are forgotten
by the strangers hearing it, unless they are folklorists. Out of sight,
out of mind.[1]

If folklore was scarce and spotty, a distinctive folkstyle took
root in the South. Unlike Washington Irving or Herman Melville,
Southerners didn't have to go to Spain or Tahiti for genuine folk
material. There it was, outside their window; a traditional society,

rural, conservative, hierarchical.

No one mirrored its inner values better than Joel Chandler Harris, an archetypal American Folklorist. Born in rural Georgia in 1848, Harris went to "Turnwold" plantation to work as a printer on a weekly paper, *The Countryman.* Surrounded by slaves, he soaked up their folk tales and mannerisms. After the Civil War, Harris moved to Atlanta and got a job on the *Constitution.* Two years later, when Samuel Small gave up a Negro dialect column which he had been writing, Harris continued it.[2] Through him the much genuine Negro folklore and legend was transmitted to the literary world. Having spent days hunting 'coons, 'possums, rabbits, and foxes, Harris knew rural life and character intimately. His friends included Uncle Remus the gardener, Uncle Bob Capers the teamster, and Uncle George Terrell the recluse. "I just walloped them together into one person and called him Uncle Remus," Harris explained. "You must remember that sometimes the Negro is a genuine and an original philosopher."[3]

Tales of animals and "creatures" were common in the Old South. James Audubon encountered them in the bayous, Opie Read in the mountains, Mark Twain along the rivers. Northern children with Southern antecedents heard them too. In his *Autobiography,* Theodore Roosevelt writes: "Aunt Anna and my Mother used to entertain us by the hour with tales of life on the Georgia plantations; of hunting fox, deer, and wildcat; and of the queer goings on in the Negro quarters. She knew all the Brer Rabbit stories, and I was brought up on them."

Folk tales of the Negroes and the Cherokee Indians intermingled. In *Myths of the Cherokees,* James Mooney shows that the Great White Rabbit is the hero-god, trickster, and wonder-worker of many tribes east of the Mississippi. The Indians regarded the rabbit as the fitting type of defenseless weakness, protected and made safe by constant vigilance. Thus many Southern stories now cherished by the white man were cherished by the black and red men before him.

Harris' tales, like *Alice in Wonderland,* are only ostensibly for children.[4] Harris himself never read or told them to his own children, and labeled them allegorical. "It takes no scientific investigation to show why the Negro selects as his hero the weakest and most harmless of all animals, and brings him out victorious," he wrote. "It is not virtue that triumphs, but helplessness; not malice, but mischievousness." His ten volumes of Uncle Remus stories are monuments to poetic justice and to mercy. We watch Brer Rabbit going to sunset prayer meeting to get himself freshened with the Lord; Brer Fox providing Brer Rabbit with firewood from sheer compassion; Brer Hawk soaring up to say "Howdy" to the sun.

On such sound material the myth of the Old South, shining and golden, could be erected. In it the region is, first and foremost, a land of enchantment. Novels and folk tales are convincing ways of depicting it. While historians check each meticulous brush stroke, creative writers capture with a few bold and bright colors the feeling and motivation of past glory.

We err in considering myths untrue renditions of the past. If not built on at least a partial framework of historical truth, they will not survive. Most myths are closer to half-formulated beliefs than to facts. As Ortega Y. Gassett points out in *Ideas y Creencias,* such beliefs rightly claim a position for historians on a par with that of ideas. The study of ideas is not merely the exposition of theoretical views, but also "the history of the deformations undergone by these ideas when other men adopt them, and also the history of the half-conscious beliefs into which ideas first clearly conceived by the few promptly transform themselves."[5] Mythology is psychology misread as history, biography, or cosmology.

People live by the mythology of their time. The medievalists had their saints, the British their empire, the philosophers their reason. America had incredible diversity (cultural, ethnic, geographical) and pockets of genuine folk culture. But it was not until the twentieth century that a unique style appeared. Entering that century first (which is why, Gertrude Stein said, America is the oldest nation on earth) we found a new mode of expression. Embodying aspects of folklore, and chunks of fakelore, it was an international style adapted to the new electronic environment. But few American folklorists had either the training or inclination to study it. Learning little from the anthropologists, who made remarkable strides forward in the years after World War II, most professional folklorists did business as

usual—and bankrupted their subject. As folk material in rural ham-
lets disappeared, they did not seek it in urban ghettoes. They
lamented the disappearance of zithers—but did not hail the electric
guitars, which took over with a vengeance. Folklore's sorry plight
is reflected in the work and pronouncements of Richard Dorson, a
combative but restricted scholar who laments:

> The cavernous maw of the mass media gobbled
> up endless chunks of folksiness, and a new ration-
> ale appeared for the folklorist: his mission is to
> polish up, revamp, and distribute folkore to the
> American people. . . . We cannot tarry with
> folklore performers and popularizers. . . .[6]

Nor can folklore tarry with the Richard Dorson's. It has and
will evolve as does the dynamic culture it mirrors. "Popularizers"
do not threaten Folklore; they provide material, arguments, trends.
In their own day Homer, Dante, Shakespeare, and the man who
added a few verses to "Barbara Allen" were popularizers. Their
spiritual descendants appear on film and tape today shaping and
leading the Pop Revolution. They and their followers—not the folklorists—keep folklore alive.

The creative thrust in folklore studies is the "folklife movement."
Adapted from the Swedish *folkliv,* the word implies an analysis of
folk culture in its entirety. By limiting themselves largely to literary
aspects of folklore, scholars have tended to slight all other aspects,
and to take the material studied out of total context. In Sweden today over 400 communities maintain "outdoor museums." The first
such venture in America was in Decorah, Iowa in 1925. The most
spectacular was Williamsburg (began in 1926 and still going strong).
Despite good work at Cooperstown, Sturbridge, Shelburne, and
Dearborn, we still know and see far too little of folklife. Professor
Don Yoder, a leading advocate of the folklife movement, lists things
we should study: folk names, agriculture, architecture, cookery,
costume, crafts, medicine, music, recreation, religion, speech, trans-
portation, the folk year. Back to the plow and the flail, the husking

peg and hominy block, the schoolhouse and meetinghouse!

Knowing more about settlement patterns, games, song, dance, clothing, and customary behavior, we might see folklore as an integral part of the total range of traditional behavior—and hence of popular culture.

We might also find new dimensions for our teaching and writing.

To illustrate: long isolated Scotch-Irish farmers in the Ozarks are so deeply Calvinistic that they still refer to bulls as "gentlemen cows" in mixed company. Yet they send maidens to dance in apple orchards each spring, and encourage couples to "jolly themselves" in newly planted fields, thus helping seeds to germinate. In the ritual for sowing flax, Vance Randolph reports, the farmer and his wife appear naked in the field at sunup. The woman walks ahead as the man sows. They chant a rhyme which ends, "Up to my ass, and higher too!" Every few steps the man throws seeds against the woman's buttocks, singing and scattering until the planting is done. "Then they just lay down on the ground and have a good time," Professor Vance concludes. A less delicate informer has this to say of turnip planting:

> The boy throwed all the seed, and the gals kept
> a-hollering "Pecker deep! Pecker deep!" And
> when they got done, the whole bunch would roll
> in the dust like wild animals. Ain't no sense to
> it, but they always raised the best turnips on the
> creek!

10. FAKELORE

I have seen the wild duck become the dead duck, and
the dead duck become Donald Duck.

—Henry Miller

Fakelore is phony folklore—manufactured, canned, and peddled
to a gullible public. It is also the link between oldstyle folklore and
newstyle poplore; the transitional phase between a genuinely rural
and a genuinely urban orientation. Without that transition Pop Culture of our time would have been impossible.

Scholars argue about when and how the transition began. "After
1860," Richard Dorson writes in *American Folklore*, "the homespun
yarn never again became nationally intelligible. A century later literary
scholars and folklorists would unearth specimens as antiquarian
curiosities." Whether or not folk or folklorists were at fault, it is
certainly true that the work of many scholars in the field smacks of
antiquarianism. Unwilling to study fakelore or poplore on equal
terms with folklore, they find their subject disappearing under their
very eyes.

A famous 1869 hoax pointed to the new day. Workmen in the
little town of Cardiff, New York "discovered" a buried petrified
figure over 10 feet tall, weighing 2,990 pounds. Carved in Iowa and
buried in New York by George Hull, the Cardiff Giant won considerable fame. Phineas T. Barnum offered $60,000 for three month's
rental. Oliver Wendell Holmes declared the giant "of wonderful

76

anatomical development," and Ralph Waldo Emerson called it "beyond my depth, very wonderful and undoubtedly ancient." Even
when Hull admitted the thing was a gigantic fake, there remained
for years those who believed in it.[1] The Gilded Age was the Golden
Age of Fakelore. *Ersatz* giants, epics, and ballads flooded the market;
journalism, advertising, and entertainment pooled their efforts and
popularized the homely, folksy, and schmaltzy. Barber shop quartets
wailed their chromatic chords. Not far down the road, the Fakelore
Kingdom called Disneyland would eventually loom large.

Exploitation of folk materials is no new thing. The Grimm
brothers discovered (among other things) a good market for fairy
tales. Poets have long imitated the ballad; pseudo-folktales and epics
are not rare. But in late nineteenth century America what Daniel G.
Hoffman calls "the dynamics of transmission" altered.[2] New mass
media began to manipulate folk opinions and to create a new "climate." An old culture was vanishing; a new one had not yet developed.
In art, architecture, literature, and social custom one finds an absorp-
tion in externalities; a cultural inferiority complex; a sentimental
nostalgia. Notice the generation gap between the elder Henry James
and his sons; between Bronson Alcott and daughter Louisa, who
peddled literary lollypops to the *nouveau riche* middle class. Nor was
Buffalo Bill's not-so-wild West Show out of tune with the 1890's.
Like *Little Women*, it too was essentially a tear-jerker.

The age is still hard to characterize. It was prudish (Victorian),
greedy (Robber Baron), vulgar (Gilded Age), frivolous (Gay Nineties),
somber (Brown Decades). Around 1900 we were confronted with a
new relationship between the people and the earth which supported
them. The old certainties went up in smoke.

The ambiguities are clearly reflected in the works of Mark Twain
and Henry Adams; the dismal vacancy in the black prose of Ambrose
Bierce. "The post-Civil War writers who deal with *Roughing It, A Son
of the Middle Border*, or *A Hoosier Schoolmaster* had already abandoned the scene of the pioneer's efforts," Lewis Mumford points out.
"They made copy of their early life, but, though they might be in-
clined to sigh after it, because it was associated with their youth, they
had only a sentimental notion of continuing it."[3]

The tendency towards exaggeration and sensational melodrama dominated sub-literary publications. Frank Murdock's *Davy Crockett* (1872) is a case in point. Trapped in Davy's cabin during a blizzard, the heroine, Eleanor, reads him the story of young Lochinvar. To keep warm they burn all the cabin furniture and the bar to the door. Only "the strong arm of a backwoodsman" keeps the wolves out; hence, sweet Eleanor ends up "happy in heart and home of Davy Crockett." Compare such lines with the earthy prose of the early Crockett almanacs. Or read David Belasco's *The Girl of the Golden West* (1905), used as the libretto of an exotic grand opera by Puccini. The blood and stench of the Old West were gone; what remained, in the mind's eye, was golden.

Although a number of people who have actually *lived* in small towns, full of folk traditions, have found them less then idyllic, the belief that rural, smalltown folk are more fortunate than the crowded sinful cities has persisted up to our own day. Exploiting this sentiment with fakey songs, artifacts, and even shrines, has gone on throughout America. Disney World is a kind of fake small town that convinces us that life was like it *should* have been, not like it really was.

What was it like? Michael Lesy tries for a documented and factual answer in his 1973 study called *Wisconsin Death Trap*. His thesis is that at the turn of the century small towns were filled with despair. The optimists had all fled to the cities; those who had nothing to live for stayed put, festered, and decayed. Does this tell us something of the seedbed in which fakelore flourished?

As a rural community becomes urbanized, it becomes less homogenous and well-integrated. Inevitably the old folklore must either adapt a new environment (as is often done without scholars recognizing it), or give way to a fakelore which preserves the forms but not the substance of earlier days.[4] Sociologist Howard Odum, noting the steady destruction of the bases of folk culture attuned to nature and ethnic structure, wanted to replace the term "folkways" with "technicways." That, in a sense, is what has happened. Call "technicways" Pop and see for yourself.

"Folk," H. W. Fowler wrote in his 1926 *Dictionary of Modern*

English Usage, "has passed out of the language of the ordinary educated person, so far as he talks unaffectedly." But phony fake demigods had just begun to take over. Three years earlier, in a 1923 issue
of *Century Magazine,* "Tex" O'Reilly had thrust Pecos Bill onto the
scene. Paul Bunyan had preceded him; Big Mose, Strap Buckner,
Annie Christmas, Bowleg Bill, Tony Beaver, Febold Feboldson, Gib
Morgan and Whiskey Jack would follow. So would one of the most
revealing examples in which the concocter was himself duped by his
informants. Who was the jackass in the case of Joe Magarac?

The chief actor in this story was Owen Francis, who grew up in
rural Pennsylvania in the early twentieth century, got gassed in World
War I, and returned home to write about "the Hunkies and Polocks
who understand life." Having toured Pennsylvania's steel mills, he
published an article on Joe Magarac for the October 1931 *Scribners,*
featuring a legendary hero who threw himself into a Bessemer
furnace to improve the quality of steel for a new mill. Like John
Henry, a genuine Folk hero, Magarac gave all he had to his people.

The martyr's death has been variously interpreted by different
interest groups. Corporation staff writers modified it so that when
the Depression came, Joe melted himself down to make better steel
for a modern mill that would produce more. Thus Joe was made to
support the industry argument that hard times are cured by more
production and lower prices. The less capitalistic Federal Writer
Project employees had Joe realize that his great strength was actually
depriving others of jobs. His solution, according to them, was to quit
and go to sleep until prosperity and employment returned. But
despite the different twists, the basic pattern was Owen Francis'.
Nothing has ever demonstrated that Magarac is an authentic folk hero,
or that Magarac stories go back beyond 1931.

Folklorists have looked into the Magarac situation and have
been unable to uncover any folk information or tradition about Joe.
Neither the Pennsylvania Historical Society nor the Pennsylvania Folklore Society have any pre-Francis items. Newspaper morgues, special
collections, and major steel corporation files are equally barren.
Editors of various Slavic and Hungarian language newspapers in the
steel belt knew nothing of Joe; most of them think it impossible that

such a hero existed among their people. Local historians and editors of Braddock, McKeesport, and Homestead—towns sometimes associated with Magarac—have never heard an oral Magarac story.

The next step is to go to the workers, union officials, and foremen, to see what they knew of Joe. Richard Hyman interviewed a hundred such informants in a dozen different towns. He spoke to those of Scotch, Irish, Swedish, Croatian, Serbian, Slovenian, Polish, Russian, Hungarian and Italian descent. The answer was always the same: "I never heard of him." "In one fortunate instance," Hyman records, "I was able to interview 42 informants, the entire supervisory staff of one of the mills. They had from 20 to 50 years of steel experience, having worked up through the ranks. Most of them had been employed in the steel mills since coming to this country. Not a single one had ever heard of Joe Magarac."[5] Even more telling was a discovery made by looking into the linguistic origins. Joe is supposed to be Hungarian, but "magarac" is not a Hungarian word, and cannot be found anywhere in the language.

The word "magarac" is Slavic, existing only in the Croatian and Serbian. It has very strong vulgar connotations, somewhat like the word "bloody" for the English. The closest English equivalent is "jackass." The Slavs never use the word without sneering. Paul Blazek, Slavic publisher, says that to call a man magarac "is to lower him to dirt that is worse than after pigs pass over it." An old time steel worker in Clairton was embarrassed when Mr. Hyman used the word in front of his wife. A moulder named Steve Berko warned him that if he called someone that he'd get his head bashed in. The Slavic steel workers probably decided to play a huge joke on the tenderfoot journalist Owen Francis. They must have been amazed to find someone so naive as to be deceived by something they reported so obviously in jest. Albert Stolpe, veteran steel worker, told an investigator "Somebody played a helluva big joke on Francis." Andrew Matta, Braddock mills craneman, thought they wanted to make a fool out of him. They not only fooled Francis, but many of his readers as well. The questions of intent and integrity are always important in judging episodes of this nature. Folklore is uncopyrighted (by definition, unwritten) material. Who can say how it should be adapted, rejuvenated, parodied? That much genuine folk material remains, by anyone's definition, is clear. During the Depression John Lomax toured the back country in his truck finding wonderful material in cotton fields and in prison farms. On the other hand the "Wayfaring Stranger" John Jacob Niles faked sources and imitated the hill people so he could live comfortably in the city. While scholars like MacEdward Leach were collecting the beautiful *Folk Ballads and Songs from the Lower Labrador Coast,* Maurice A. Jagendorf was mass-producing anthologies which (said his publisher) were "overflowing with excitement and crammed with laughs." His *New England Bean-Pot, Sand in the Bag,* and *Marvelous Adventures of Johnny Darling* are examples of folk-fake fusion.

One likes to think that such mish-mashing was often accidental —or at least not put forward as a hoax. We like to feel that fakelore is a form of escapism—as when during the 1930's millions of Americans flocked to movie houses to see Shirley Temple sail off on the good ship *Lollypop,* or Judy Garland follow the Yellow Brick Road to the Land of Oz.

We are less happy, however, when books like George Grotz's *Instant Furniture Refinishing and Other Crafty Practices* appear, with this statement: "What I am unabashedly proposing here is the raising of cheating to the level of an art form."[6] Who can enjoy Clifford Irving's book on *Fakes,* followed by his own fake biography of Howard Hughes, which (since it also involved swindling) sent both Irving and his wife to jail? And suppose one of the two major political party fakes an honest campaign while practicing dishonesty on various fronts and levels?

Fakelore is for popular culture the dark side of the moon. It raises questions as deep and disturbing as the nature of man himself —and of man's inhumanity to man. Consider the much-heralded fake "religious revival" of the 1950's. Was it not only a product of and tool for the shrewd manipulators (of and outside the cloth) whose God could fly no higher than the American dollar? And isn't the "Ersatz West" exemplified in promotor-built "Old Tuscon," where shoot-outs are staged on announced schedules, less than amusing? Are we not on the verge of the dilemma presented in Anon

Chekhov's short story, "The Hollow":

> You remember, before the wedding, Anisim
> brought me some new rubles and half rubles?
> I hid one packet, the rest I mixed with my own.
> Now I can't make out which is real money and
> which is counterfeit. It seems they are all false
> coins. I'm frightened. I can't be well.

11. MOSAICS

Everything descends upon us from everywhere all at once.

—Marshall McLuhan

Now, the world is neither meaningful nor absurd. It simply is.

—Alain Robbe-Grillet

First it was Brave New World; then Seedbed of Empire; then the Promised Land. That promise, attracting millions of tempest-tossed immigrants, created the Melting Pot. As it bubbled and boiled, politicians kept throwing in fresh labels: New Freedom, New Deal, New Frontier. For many growing up today, America means none of these things.

To some, it is a haphazard happening; to others, a series of well-planned pseudo-events; to others a king-sized sound-and-light show or spectacle. Will the real America stand up?

On some points, those who hold the three opinions share common ground. All refuse to endorse "onward and upward," as did Grandad in Bull Moose days, or "downward and out," as did Dad during Depression and Doom Boom. News—coming from everywhere instantly—is neither logical nor illogical but alogical. Politics is a kind of pop art-form, the planet a king-size art-object. Six words sum it up best: now, pop, fluid, action, accidental, cool. "The present instant," writes George Kubler, "is the plane upon which the signals of all being are projected."

"They are simply shallow and ignorant," the antique and learned complain. Lack of historical perspective and the telescoping of time have been alarming human failings for centuries. Unwilling or unable to reach valid conclusions from inconclusive evidence, men have long preferred to be hysterical to historical. But the term hysterical does not characterize the current youthful attitude. Rather than being hot and involved, they are cool and detached. They do not despair, they tune in.

First popularized by Allan Kaprow in 1959, the word "Happening" involves a spontaneous, unrehearsed, and often unconnected cluster of events; a sequence of unstructured and largely unrelated paradoxes that will not resolve; dilemmas that will not dissolve. Richard Schechner says Happenings are rooted in two seemingly unrelated interests: (1) an attempt to bring into a celebratory space the full "message-complexity" of a downtown street and (2) a playing with modes of perception. Built on "chance" techniques, Happenings relieve everyone of the burden of choosing when to do something. They stress multi-focus, non-characterized (the new term is non-matrixed), non-definite relationship between play and audience. If a circus were a work of art, it would be the perfect example of a Happening. No information structure is implied. Every act in each ring is a thing in itself. Yet taken together, the events make a total performance which is more than the sum of its parts.

One errs in equating Happenings with such historical predecessors as the Absurd theatre, Artaud, Surrealism, and Dada, which concentrated on the message received, the thing done. Happenings are vitally concerned with those who do and those who witness. Hence they can never be predicated, repeated, or evaluated on paper. Artists can no longer work in isolation since they confront a group on either side of their message. Everything is interdependent. In some instances audience and performer merge. Who is what in a Theatre Game or an Activity? Where will Claes Oldenburg's Ray

Gun Theatre, Carolee Schneemann's Kinetic Theatre, Ken Dewey's Action Theatre, and Ann Halprin's Once Group take us? Happenings!

And what factual happenings we have—President Kennedy shot down by an ex-marine with a mail order rifle; then the man who shot him killed on the TV screen. High-level Republican officials bugging Democratic headquarters at Watergate—a domino-theory of involvement removed from foreign affairs and put squarely in the White House. The longest, most bitter war in American history waged against a small agricultural nation in southeast Asia; a Space-lab sent into orbit, too hot for the space men to enter. Happenings!

The notion of irrationality dominates not only the news but the gallery and theater in recent years. Instead of form and structure in plays, pictures, and structures, we got syntax, colors, and objects jumbled beyond recognition. In the world of Samuel Beckett, one of the generation's most admired playwrights, men sit on nothing identifiable, existing in a gray space. The whole world crawls from left to right along an invisible track. One character resembles the square root of 2. Happenings!

Eugene Ionesco's *The Chairs* is concerned with the absence of people, of matter, and of God. In Edward Albee's *The Sandbox* the Angel of Death parades by in a bikini. *The Blacks,* by Jean Genet, depicts three cloaked black men who imitate whites. (This kind of race-switching occurs in comic books, films, and social dating. Whatever the "old generation" found unbelievable will, by the new Law of Popular Culture, become the new fad.) The zanier the better. For example, the Butcher in Arnold Weinstein's *The Red Eye of Love* busies himself building a skyscraper out of used meat.

In the Theatre of the Absurd we get (to quote Richard Barr) "a distorted picture of a world that has gone mad—in order to break the old mold of language and narrative sequence in the theatre and to emphasize the mystery and truth." Edward Albee puts it this way: "Man attempts to make sense out of his senseless position in a world that makes no sense. The social structures man has erected to illusion himself have collapsed." The result, on every level, is the happening . . . "would you believe?" That this idea has permeated the world of Everyman is obvious. "Expect the unexpected" is more than a cliche; it is a guidepost for living.

Another group, convinced that the new atmosphere is not accidental but arranged, insist that the key to American society is the pseudo-event. The germinal statement here is Daniel Boorstin's in *The Image* (1962). Forty years earlier, in *Public Opinion,* Walter Lippman had distinguished between "the world outside and the pictures inside our head"; and centuries earlier Plato had warned the pictures on the cave wall were easily confused with reality. The new factor that has complicated image-making is electronic technology and speed. Consequently the new instantaneous image-making has spilled over into politics, art, journalism, and education. The result is extravagant expectations. We expect anything and everything-heroes every season, best sellers every month, TV spectaculars every week, a rare sensation every night.

No improvement of instruments for making and receiving images can keep up with such expectations; the only answer is pseudo-events. This, Boorstin and his followers claim, is the basis of popular culture, and images have become the pseudo-events of the ethical world.

What is a "pseudo-event"? One planned or planted to be reported and reproduced. Never spontaneous, it is given out in advance "for future use." A self-fulfilling prophecy is attached. By saying the event is significant, we tend to make it so.

Pseudo-events are more dramatic than reality, being planned with that in mind. They can be repeated, and thus reinforced, at will. They are also more sociable and convenient than reality; knowing about them is the test of being "in." Pseudo-events spawn other such events in geometric fashion. A new Gresham's law shapes up in the public arena; counterfeit happenings will always drive spontaneous ones out of circulation.

When the gods want to punish us, they make us believe our own news releases and politicians.

Such a definition of pseudo-events and procedures allows us to distinguish between the American dream (a noble thing) and the American image (an ignoble con job). The nation becomes infected with a dread disease, social narcissism. When he jilted the mountain nymph Echo, Narcissus was condemned to fall in love with his own image. Obsessed with the view of himself in the water, he stayed on, transfixed, to die of languor. In this comparison we are, as a nation, Narcissus. Having jilted Echo (the real American dream), we have fallen in love with images of ourselves.

What then are the images we get in the mass media? They are self-images or self-fantasies. The situation comedies are amusing quintesences of our own slightly absurd lives. So saying, we have come back to the essentially elitist viewpoint: whatever everybody likes is necessarily bad. Whatever prevails in our mass society is, by definition, absurd; our scientific gadgets have led us into the ultimate *cul de sac.*

The Pseudo-Eventists have popularized an old and vigorous line of Western thought which currently goes under the label of Existentialism. Some claim its origins are rooted in the ancient Greeks; others that it springs from early poets like François Villon, and after him Rabelais and Montaigne; still others see it as a reaction against the rationalism that dominated Western thought from Descartes through Hegal. Whatever its origins, it has spilled out of the philosophic mold into literature, drama, theology, history, and mass media. Existentialism, in the rather loose sense in which it is used here, is not so much a system as a protest against systematizing. Particularly in the physical sciences, "laws" and "certainties" of the Newtonian world have been superseded. "To what appeared to be the simplest question," J. Robert Oppenheimer writes in *Science and the Common Understanding,* "we now tend to give either no answer or an answer which will at first sight sound like a strange catechism."

This "strange catechism" attempts to analyze the great emptiness of modern life; the nothingness that lies curled at the heart of being like a worm. Existence is action and involvement. Haunted by the gnawing passion to thwart meaninglessness, man gravitates toward ruts, pigeonholes, and fantasies. "Stop it!" existentialists cry. "Only when you struggle are you human. The uncommitted life isn't worth living."

The real enemy is inauthentic existence. Its hallmarks are

abstractions, circumlocutions, pomposity. Meaning emerges only in
the struggle between creativity and inquisition. "A creative period
in art," Albert Camus wrote, "can be defined as an order of style
applied to the disorder of an age." And again, in a poignant
description of modern man's plight: "I have always felt that I lived
on the high seas, menaced, at the heart of a royal happiness."

Existentialism's diagnosis has striking relevance in contemporary America. Wrapped in an ethnocentric cocoon, we find ourselves
acting as if today's values were permanent fixtures. We are serious
about trivialities (electric toothbrushes, sports cars, hair-dos), trivial
about reality (life, encounter, death). We insist on convenient
categorical pegs on which to hang every conception; despise un-
certainty and disorder; and impose both certainty and order where
none exists. So it is in suburbia, the market place, the university.
Instead of real education we offer adjustment, pressing pliant human
beings into patterns, filling curricula with supermarket knowledge
conveniently packaged and labeled. Pat answers masquerade as truth.
Some bewildered intellectuals have retreated to the eighteenth century's excessive adulation for reason. Fighting flux with formalism,
they are reconciled to superficiality in every phase of life. And having only one life to live, our frightened females decide they might as
well live it as a blonde.

We accord ultimate meaning to the useful, but refuse to ask,
useful for what? Increasingly we find ourselves being transformed
into things—cogs in the universal system of organized production
and consumption. We tend to be lonely in crowds, trapped in or-
ganizations, entranced by status symbols. Life seems like getting a
mailbag full of second-class matter. Hence W. H. Auden's caustic
invitation:

> Come to our well run desert
> Where anguish comes by cable
> And the deadly sins can be bought in tins
> With instructions on the label.

In more and more areas of American life the ability or even advisability of stating airtight theories and infallible propositions is being questioned. Better honest doubt than dishonest certainty. Thus Robert A. Dahl describes the contemporary concept of power:

> We are not likely to produce—certainly not for some considerable time to come—anything like a consistent, coherent "theory." We are much more likely to produce a variety of theories of limited scope, each of which employs some definition that is useful in the context of the particular piece of research or theory but different in important respects from the definitions of other studies.

This viewpoint has also been expressed by "realists" in political theory—Reinhold Niebuhr, Walter Lippmann, Hans Morgenthau, George Kennan, and Kenneth Thompson. Learn to resist the great American impatience; live with ambiguities and avoid generalizations. Look behind the verbiage for real issues and positions. Make possibilities the function of actuality; but never consider actuality the only possibility.

In a more bizarre and less articulate way, Beats, hipsters, Freaks, and sick comedians make the same basic points. Disgusted with a slick, sentimental, cultural veneer, they stand outside the culture, just as existential dramatists are off Broadway. The Outsider theme, stretching back to the days of Job, Ulysses, and Beowulf, seems to have special relevance and poignancy in our time. Being "way out" has replaced being "in" as the expression of social acceptance. In the world of intellect, externalism has become an established orthodoxy.

There is a crudity, even savagery, in some popular culture which startles and appalls us. The roots are deep. As the transcendentalist Geroge P. Marsh pointed out a century ago, America provides "a notable example of the struggle between civilized man and barbarous uncultivated nature. Our cultural hero is the savage,

his theater is the wilderness." Marsh may have been thinging of
Deerslayer; but we can find an equally valid example in *Shaft,* the
Copslayer.

The task of this hero, and even its best poets, is (in Whitman's
words) to "take the hinges off the door." There is something not
only dynamic, but almost satanic, in our popular culture; breaking
out and breaking in . . . going west and coming east . . . moving
up and down the social ladder. In Old World cities, buildings cluster
like sheep and protect one another against open space. But in New
York, observes Jean-Paul Sartre, "Your streets are not sober little
walks closed in between houses, but national highways. The moment
you set foot in one of them, you understand that they go on to
Boston or Chicago." What is basically "American" is the concern
with process as reflected in the work of heads, hearts, and hands.
By what process do we create instant slums, colonial villages, neon
nightmares, Jesus freaks, Watergates? What have we here?

A land of atomic reactors, foot-long hot dogs. Charles Addams
Gothic, Hopi Indians, imitation castles, guided missiles, block slums,
freedom marches, glass domes, mobile homes, little magazines, big
sells, wetbacks, flashbacks, comebacks.

A land dotted with names to set a poet musing—Dry Bones,
Nantucket, Go-to-Hell Gulch, Lost Mule Flat, Machopongo, Bubble-
up, Wounded Knee, Roanoke, Purgatory Creek, Lake June in Winter,
Okaloacoochee Slough, and Boot Hill. A continent of sharp, bright
cold and sapping heat, fit to grow corn, wheat, weeds, and a new
language of film.

Film is not only a substance but a process. It allows one to
use form, color, movement, space, time, and sound all at once; to
produce a reality separate from real life. Literature, drama, music,
painting, dance, and photography—and any variation of them—can
be put into the mix. The "commercial film" has become "underground films," personal statements by one person, became another
potent force for interpretation and expression.

Film blends time, space and memory into immediate projection.
"Our movies are like extensions of our own pulse, of our heartbeat,
or our eyes, or fingertips," Jonas Mekas writes. "We want to sur-

round this earth with our film frames and warm it up—until it begins to move."

The spectacle of which I speak is far removed from the stately masque of Tudor England, or the mannered formality of a pageant at Versailles. In the electronic spectacle, sounds smells sights inundate—squawks and squeaks like the short-wave radio from Vladivostok in a storm. Bang bang big-beat, hailstones falling and bodies starting to grind. Echoing electronic chambers, raw melodies riding computers bareback.

The spectacle is protean, readily assuming new shapes and roles. De Tocqueville's "motley Multitude" seems to have gone mad.

Where may you see it? At a rock concert or electric lightshow, of course; but also on a busy Times Square, a super-market during special sales, any beach on July 4th, any good variety show on TV.

There are elements of all these things (happenings, pseudo-events spectacles) in our culture; but the word that describes it best is *mosaics.* They are made by inlaying pieces of various material— enamel, glass, marble, mother-of-pearl—so as to produce a flow rather than a sequence. The bits and pieces create a complex multi-level awareness and participation. The moment one sets up a mosaic he's already touching. Juxtapositions require touch.

The extraordinary efflorescence of mosaic art has long been admired and acknowledged. "One might say," Guiseppe Bovini writes, "that light is multiplied because as it strikes the surface it is automatically split into an infinite number of chromatic units."[1] For me this is not only an apt description of a Byzantine wall, but of contemporary American society.

No wonder an unknown poet, overwhelmed by the mosaics on entering the Church of San Vitale in Ravenna, wrote:

AUT LUX NATA EST ET CAPTA HIC LIBERA REGNANT
(Either light was born or captured and freed here)

No wonder Dante, writing portions of *The Divine Comedy* in mosaic-filled Ravenna, wrote:

And flashing from the flowers with hues intense
Like very rubies from gold patinas gleaming.

The flashing, the intensity, the gleaming: you may have felt
them when a fire truck or ambulance speeds by . . . when a
satellite leaves its pad at Cape Kennedy . . . when Elvis Presley
sings in front of all the klieg lights . . . when you see a large city at
night, swooping down from the air.

Or you may have marveled at the master mosaics of word-ar-
rangers like James Joyce, William Faulkner, William Burroughs,
Kurt Vonnegut. *Let us swim freestyle in a verbal sea.*

Can such mosaics be our model, our method, our metaphor?

Saying *yes* is one thing; mosaic-making is another. For some
time I have felt the urge to make mosaics—and thus to open up a
new path for studying and presenting popular culture. In a classroom,
where words, sounds, images, and even smells can be utilized, I have
had some success. But how to translate this onto white paper with
black ink?

How can verbal pellets, or tesserae, be assembled so as to
produce the new effect we seek? I am still working on the problem,
stock-piling the tesserae for future use. From this "work in progress,"
let me show you four samples—those on *Dance, Disney, Jazz*, and
Trinity:

DANCE
After Eisenhower, popular dancing broke out of its boxstep
with a savage, revolutionary intensity. True enough, the natives had
long clicked their heels, and there had been a bit of Truckin', Peckin',
and Big Apple. But what had prepared us for the Twist, that Brave
New Whirl? And who would have thought that one's dance partner
would soon become as distant as friendly meetings on the other side
of the Berlin Wall or Iron Curtain?

DISNEY
This essentially is Dreamworld: in living color, 3-D, sanitized,
simplified, souped up. And what do you make of its creator? Dirty

Old Man!
Disneyland blossomed into Disney World. Supergrow, super-fun, super-profit. By reservation only . . . this too is part of the American dream.

JAZZ
It is old hat now, but still Hot Stuff.
"I remember nights when we didn't go down to the bomb shelter because we listened to jazz records," the German pianist Jutta Hipp wrote after World War II. "We had the feeling that you are not our enemies. Even though the bombs crashed around us, we felt safe."
The implications of such statements—they can be found around the world—are social and psychic, as well as musical.
"Jazz shows us the image of the 20th century man, in search of his humanity," writes Professor Wilson Wade. Styles come and go—Dixie, ragtime, swing, bop, West Coast, cool—but jazz remains in the main stream. That is because it is the valid symbol for the renewed affirmation we so desperately need.
"To swing," writes a Jesuit priest at Loyola University (Father Kennard), "is to affirm."
"Where lucidity reigns," Albert Camus wrote, "a scale of values becomes unnecessary."

TRINITY
I speak not of Father, Son, and Holy Ghost, but the popular and powerful substitutes:

The Bomb	all-powerful father of our policies, capable of destroying all the children.
The Pill	no son when this prevails: does zero population equal no go?
The Tube	ghostly images filling our rooms, our lives, our thoughts: Holy Moses!

And all these items relatively small and manageable. One hand can carry a hundred pills; one man a TV set; one small plane a bomb. Small—and yet, what a falling off is there!

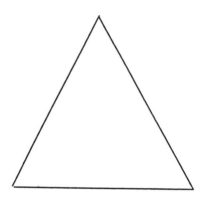

Who will master Media Mosaics, and turn the rest of us on?

12. THEOLOGY

God is not essentially religious.

—Archbishop William Temple

This is the message of Pop Theology: God is neither *in* hand (sunny assumption of romantic optimists) nor *out* of hand (gloomy contention of romantic pessimists) but *at* hand. Confronted with a 7-day work week, He can't spend all His time hovering around altars. The church had better get with it. There's no more room in the womb.

In the summer of 1955 Thomas J. J. Altizer was reading an essay on Nietsche in the University of Chicago Library. Things started unraveling. "I knew that God was dead," he later wrote. "If faith can but whisper in our world, it can take a step toward life. And we can never take that step until we know that God is Dead. We can say with thanksgiving, God is Dead. Thank God."

Theological observers like to call this moment the great recent break-through.[1] They need to look back at Nazi Germany to a prison camp when a young priest named Diedrich Bonhoeffer wrote:

> Honesty demands that we recognize that we
> must live in a world as if there were no God.
> And this is just what we do recognize—
> before God! God himself drives us to this
> realization—God makes us know that we must

95

live as men who can get along without Him.

In the years since Bonhoeffer was martyred, the main thrust of
theology has turned from dreams of New Jerusalem to the reality of
Secular City. Existentialism has become the predominant force in
contemporary philosophy. Both trends are paralleled by developments in Pop Culture; the same laser-beam light illuminates them all.

Pilgrim makes his progress in today's world not on foot with a
staff but in a batmobile.

This is not to imply that theology is an "in" subject. For everyman, it's out. The intellectuals who have pre-empted theology have
a language and logic all their own. Dad isn't listening. He's in the
TV room, watching football. The kids? They've got the phonograph up to jet-engine decibels, listening to the New Group and doing
the new dance.

Before we see how things are with the tube and the turntable,
let's ask what the theologians have been saying and doing lately.

Twentieth century theology has been largely a housewrecking
operation. Smug sentimental doctrines of the nineteenth century—
which fostered imperialism, romantic Christianity, and simplistic
answers—have been rejected. On the other hand, there is the
pioneering work of tough-minded nineteenth century thinkers like
Soren Kierkegaard (1813-1855). This melancholy Dane was tortured
alike by doubt and doubting faith; lacerated by the sense of sin.
Ancient man, Kierkegaard noted, contended with fate; medieval
man with sin; and modern man with meaninglessness. Once you
discard all the corny cliches, what is left? (This, by the way, is
precisely the question pop painters are raising in a different context.)
What of "law and order" is left after Nixon?

To isolate, define, and if possible dispel that meaninglessness
has been a job with A-1 priority. In carrying it out, old myths and
traditions have been discarded, and new ones have taken their
place. Such transition is always painful, confusing, and controversial.
Pop culture is part of that transition.

People live by the mythology of their time. Every age is
credulous in its own way. How could our distant ancestors ever

believe that heaven and earth were made out of a severed egg, heaven being the shell and earth the yoke? Or (moving centuries forward, to the Middle Ages) that angels danced on the heads of needles and children could fight crusades? Or (jumping to Bull Moose days) that progress was inherent and White Man's Burden a Christian calling? Yet we must not be too smug. How long before a new generation asks, "Did you really believe you were splitting atoms, and that Picasso was avant garde?"

The reason Pop culture has a *WOW* impact on theology is that the present void of belief must and will be filled. The old religious symbols no longer work and cannot be made to work on a conscious level. "The stammering helplessness of the contemporary church," writes J. B. Priestly in *Literature and Western Man*, "is proof that they are now among the institutions captured by our society; compelled to follow every lunatic course it takes."

No charge could be more devastating. To the Christian the whole world is a symbol of God's creative power. God symbolized Himself into the world—incarnated Himself. The sign of the eternal Christ revealed in history is the man Jesus. The Divine as love is the only theme adequate to the cosmic symphony. New Testament parables are, on one level, symbolic stories. The sacraments are special symbolic acts which Christ understood and started or (if they were already started) blessed. The only non-symbolic thing we can say about God is that He is symbolic.

What happens to a religion or a society when the symbols stop symbolizing? If the symbols are dead, what's alive?

Reaction against the "God is Dead" position has started, and will grow in the years ahead. But the central point involved will never be erased. Theology is no longer the "queen of the sciences," or even the reservoir of faith and hope. Major theologians (Cox, Bultmann, Robinson) have been, and are, among us. But the central position of the traditional church has been abandoned.

New thinkers, like Harvey Cox, have urged churchmen to seek God in the Secular City.[2] Despite their work, the endless argument about the "sacred" and "secular" world goes on, sapping the church's already waning strength. How can man separate sacred and secular, when they are both God's? The sacred always goes bad unless it is working with the secular; the word becomes mere vapor unless it becomes flesh. There is no theology without a sociology. No matter how pure and ethereal a religion may be at first, it is always converted into something else.

Realizing this, a group of tough-minded thinkers called Existentialists have forced us to think about ultimate problems. Are we free? Have we ever been free? What does it mean to exist now, genuinely?

The golden thread of thought goes back to Plato, who pondered essences, and Aristotle, who stressed existence. That to him was reality. Man is as he does; action justifies life. Existence is action and involvement.

Pop Culture, with all its faddish stunts, asks these same questions, in a new idiom. New sounds and stagings penetrate the modern condition, ridiculing outworn dogmas and platitudes. There are many different ways and levels on which existential concern can be shown. Our cultural package is all of a piece. Change seems most radical in some areas only because we know more about them, or are more involved with them. The radical common denominator is that we accept change as a normal condition.

Abstract art affects existentialist thought, and vice versa. "Cool" music has its counterpart in "cool" architecture, styles, and diplomacy. The pieces in our kaleidoscopic culture are changing constantly, but the pieces continue to form patterns. Art borrows its motifs and devices from mass media and gives them back with interest.

Though its protest is more formal, and to the traditionalist more profound, Existentialism is simply one set of tiles in the complex mosaic we are trying to understand. *Dubito, ergo sum.*

From Descartes through Hegel western thought was dominated by rationalism system-building and the notion of progress. As in formal theology, house-wrecking has been the order of the day. Dominant themes of twentieth century philosophy are disillusionment, pessimism, and the lure of destruction. Paradox prevails: we live at a moment of economic optimism, but moral collapse.

Automation, computerization, nuclear fission, and rocketry should have made us free—but have only tyrannized us to a degree unparalleled in history. Our ancestors thought we would, by now, have built the Brave New World. Instead we seem unable to prevent blowing the old one up.

The time for grand Utopian schemes and the old "blah blah words," has passed. The general predicament must be confronted in every particular situation. Instead of being anti-religious, the Existentialists represent an ultimate religious concern—far more telling than many who grind out Sunday School literature or dignify pulpits. Man is a born phony, full of bad faith. He dodges responsibilities on all levels. Like the dishonest dentist he is content to make his living by disguising decay.

Terrified by the threat of meaninglessness we retreat into anonymity. Life becomes bearable but routine; like getting second class mail without a name. Another escape is nostalgia, with syrupy talk of the good old days. Rainier Maria Rilke spoke scornfully of such deception in the *Valais Quatrains*:

> Everything here sings the life of yesterday
> But not in a way which would destroy
> tomorrow. . . .
> It is the land which rests in its image
> And which consents to its first day.

A harsher view of the "return to the womb" emerges from Franz Kafka's *Die Verwanglung*. His hero becomes a man-sized insect who eats anything rotten. Here is an unforgettable depiction of the sense of being cast out—*das Ausgestossensein*—which is echoed in German writers like Ernest Junger, Hermann Hesse, and Heinrich Boll. Anyone who finds modern painting or sculpture grotesque or exaggerated should read their work and that of other young Europeans. He will find the same themes, tensions, and even situations which others have put on canvas or turned into tortured metal and clay.

Martin Buber, the century's leading Jewish philosopher, spoke

on "life on the narrow ridge." Driven from Europe by Hitler, dis-
inherited for his anti-Zionist opinions in Israel, Buber was a one-
man Lost Tribe roaming the world. Yet he knew his life was not
only a problem but a mystery. (Problems can be solved; mysteries,
never.) Real living is meeting. Authentic selfhood results only from
the I-Thou encounter. To turn "thou" into "it" is to deny person-
hood, and cut the heart out of life. Life is more than objective vs.
subjective; it can be transjective as well.

"My role is not to transform the world, nor man," wrote Albert
Camus, the Existentialist novelist. "For that I have not virtues
enough, nor clearsightedness. It consists in serving, where I can,
those few values without which a world, even transformed, is not
worth living in; without which a man, even new, would not be
worthy of respect." What sort of art, music, movies, and television
might result from people who opted to "serve those few values"
which captured Camus? Some of the evidence is in; *verbal* Existentialism has found an outlet in the *visual* world.

By the mid-1960's there were signs that the influence of Existentialists (especially in America) was waning. Failure to weld ethical meaning into their analysis caused many intellectuals to look
elsewhere for new inspiration. The work of Jean Paul Sartre, in
particular, shows how Existentialism, a good servant of the life of
faith, makes a poor master. Its proponents are always anthropocen-
tric, often egocentric. Like medieval monks they prefer to turn
their backs on the world rather than to struggle.

Though they do not give final answers, Existentialists raise
critical questions. Tough-minded thinkers for turbulent times, they
achieve ultimate importance by refusing to give final answers. They
collate the intellectual backdrop against which Pop Culture is being
staged.

What about Christianity's "great tradition"? Separating traditional and experimental implies that revelation is finished. If yesterday's tradition alone is to be preserved, the church will emerge as
the religious safe-deposit box where archaic images and ideas are
stored. While some segments of the church collect and horde such
treasures the secular world is where the action is.

Isn't orthodox Christianity, as revealed through the Gospels, a kind of Happening? Why should God have broken through the web of history by appearing in a minor Roman province as a Jewish carpenter? Why should He have been conceived of a virgin, rejected by his own people, and hung on a cross? Was ever a holy story more astounding (to the unbeliever, absurd) than this? Weren't the early critics right when they claimed that if the Christians ate his very flesh in the Eucharist they were self-professed cannibals?

As to astounding stories, myths, and claims, Christians have been in the forefront of history for twenty centuries. Why do they falter and turn to the conventional now?

Still not convinced? You find Pop smutty and disgusting, and Happenings ridiculous? Have you ever wondered how disgusting it must have seemed to the well-bred to have a Messiah born amidst animal-droppings in a stable; how ridiculous to have such a child proclaimed the Son of God? Christianity is based on that earthy Happening in Bethlehem. Twenty centuries later much modern art is manger art because (thank God) there is no room for it in the inn.

To say that Poplore is "incarnational" seems far-fetched to some, ridiculous to others. The word "incarnation" is out, but it is precisely the word we need. If God is working His purpose out, why should He be turned off by color TV? If He could get through the first, fifth, and eighteenth centuries, why should He cop out in the twentieth?

While old-style theologians are mourning the death of values in the world they once understood (for the neo-Puritan, Poplore is the lash of the Lord laid upon the ungodly—Satan unleashed in the discotheque) the Age of Circuitry is letting its light shine on all men. The shining light—epiphany! God is Dead only for those who seek Him in a square Tomb. He's definitely alive for those watching the Tube.

13. MYTHOLOGY

Not only is God dead, but try getting a plumber on
weekends.

–Woody Allen

Heed the heady words of Woody. Not only our plumbers but
our symbols have stopped working. We are not only demoralized—
we are also demythologized. Ancient myths and tales that sustained
us for centuries are suddenly "out." Naturally this means the generation gap is in—and growing all the time. Can we put our plumber's
wrench to "myth" and "gap" and connect them to popular culture?

Myths are glimpses of essences; they illuminate god, men, and
society. Melville called them "luminous scenes grasped in flashes of
intuition and printed on the poet's mind." Yet myth is an unconscious rather than a conscious fiction. The primitive mind isn't aware
of the meaning of its own creations. "Mythic" implies an instant
vision of an enduring truth. We heed them or perish.

Myths, like everything else, have time indexes. When asking
what people think about the *Iliad* or *Gilgamesh,* we must know *what*
people, and *when.* To understand what has happened to myth, is to
ask what has happened to time. "At electric speeds," writes Marshall
McLuhan, "we can't avoid being mythic in every gesture. The Now
contains all past, including the most primal and primitive modes.
Electronic man is older than the fish." We are not only discovering
a new mythos; we are participating in it.

The Myth Tree has been withering throughout the 20th century. A key date is June 16, 1904: the date pinpointed and dissected in James Joyce's *Ulysses*, and for me the birth date of popstyle. By splintering spelling and sequences, this epical book forced us to re-evaluate experience. In it he stated the First Law of Popular Culture: "My producers are they not my consumers?" The book was published in 1922—the same year that T. S. Eliot's *The Wasteland* told what a culture was like when the myths died:

> He who was living. . . .

in his 1922 poem was bone-dry:

> He who was living is now dead
> We who were living are now dying
> With a little patience
> Here is no water but only rock
> Rock and no water but only rock.

Other things withered, as the unchallenged "leader role" of America (especially in Europe) was everywhere challenged. The "modern" world, as understood by Locke, Jefferson, Voltaire, and Eisenhower, gave way to a post-modern world. The arts pointed the way. Daniel French gave way to Alexander Calder, John Singer to Jackson Pollock, Stephen Foster to Dizzie Gillespie. We left the world of Descartes and Newton, with closed boxes, for that of Einstein and Wernher von Braun, with infinitely open spaces. The structure of society, the order of ideas, the basic concepts of space and time were up-ended. Where there had been time-honored myth, suddenly there was a void. Even the existence of God was questioned. The church found itself in the embarrassing position of having within its affluent confines everything it needed—except God.

There is no theology without sociology; no mythology without archetypes—original patterns on which all things of the same type are modelled. Present in the unconscious though of the individual they control ways of perceiving reality. Western Man is himself a sort of archetype; mobile, optimistic, materialistic, non-aesthetic, amoral. His trademark is energy, his goal is power. We confront him as Faust, Ahab, or Frank Cowperwood; as Matt Dillon, Steve Canyon, Dylan, or Agent 007. As comic strip writers and TV producers know, the outer style changes but the inner questions remain. The what and why of man are the mysteries, even as the who and how alter and accelerate.

Updating and refurbishing our archetypes is critical. They do more to protect and justify us than all our atomic weapons.

Consider America's archetypal Eden, the frontier. Ever since Frederick Jackson Turner announced in his famous 1893 paper that it was "closed," historians have repeated his pronouncements as if they were Holy Writ. No one would dismiss Turner's thesis. But why are we so loathe to amend and extend it? The frontier spirit did not die once it reached the Pacific. After some hesitation and con-fusion it turned around and headed back towards the Atlantic. Increasingly the crowded city, not the open wilderness, cries out for heroism and originality. America's frontier is no longer along the Colorado and the Columbia, but the Potomac and the Hudson.

In mythic memory the Southern planter and Western sodbuster are romantic figures to contemplate (especially when the planter wears a Rebel uniform and the sodbuster a Cowboy sombrero). The most important fact about them is not that they existed, but that they did not prevail. It was the less glamorous but dynamic Yankee, bolstered by ever-improving technology, who accumulated wealth and power. Lament it if you will—but admit it. Then note that not only the fate of America, but much of the world, depends on our ability to build and live in tightknit interdependent urban clusters. If cities are (as Frank Lloyd Wright insisted) "Man traps," we must learn how to live and find freedom in them. Power has accumulated not only in New York and Washington, but in Moscow, Peking, Calcutta, Tokyo, Warsaw, and Havana. To the extent that America pioneered in tech-nological and architectural phases of urban life, we helped establish an archetypal democratic city-civilization. But, you say, our cities aren't civilized. Precisely—that is why the new frontier bleeds nightly in Harlem, North Philadelphia, and South Chicago.

Man against the beast—not only the beast within him, but the beast riding in the back of the police car, trained, ready to leap and (if necessary) to kill. Will today's police dog become as critical as the sheriff's horse a century ago in maintaining human decency? Or will zebras learn to respect one another's stripes, be they black or white? Can we rebuild and retool in technopolis?

This question need not dismay us, any more than retooling for a new automotive age need terrify Detroit technicians. No one is asking or expecting us to give up our archetypes, our "way of life." When car manufacturers move engines to the rear, the cars still go forward. We may abandon the killer-tactics of the tiger, and still survive and prosper in the complex new jungle.

America's technician mentality shapes not only her assembly lines and vending machines, but all aspects of her culture. Apply that mentality to painting and sculpture and Pop Art emerges.

Technology creates its own sense of time: dynamism is built into the model. Change becomes an annual ritual, a confirmed habit, an absolute. Innovation is the rule. Styles hardly come in before they move out. Color me Culture Lag.

The technician mentality abandons traditional notions of myth. Transcendence can't be put on a blueprint or flow chart. The power that technology puts into men's hand is matched only by lack of understanding as to its meaning. "In our new society," Scott I. Paradise writes in *Christians in a Technological Era,* "our old attitudes, assumptions, and theories are so inadequate that they are dangerous." Just as it is risky to repair electrical fixtures without understanding electricity, so is it folly to play with new social forces without understanding their meaning. "I find myself hard put to think of one first rate theological mind in America who has dedicated his life to studying the meaning of technology," writes Mr. Paradise. Might this help explain our lack of viable mythology? And the turn to the occult, irrational, and emotional by the children of technocrats?

Such a question points up a baffling paradox. For years the cultural goal has been "making it." But at the very moment it's "made," all meaning disappears. Popular culture here is very close to classical theology: "Vanity of vanities, said the Preacher. . . ."

Our ancestors thought we would, by now, have built the brave new world. Instead, we seem bent on blowing it up.

We must touch new godheads. Think how mythology could be enriched by encompassing electronic ecology which studies the inter-relationship of organisms in the whole Gobal Village. Until recently, ecology was largely the bailiwick of biologists concentrating on plant environments. Now ecologists see total environment not only as physical and biotic, but cultural and conceptual. Material from the traditional humanities, arts, social sciences is included. Only inter-disciplinary efforts can focus on the holistic man, who is moving into an era of *total environment* and new styles. Confronted with that movement, mythmakers have three alternatives; change, adapt, or retreat into pedantic triviality.

If only yesterday's heroes and saints are revered, in capitol and cathedral, the government and church will emerge as the safedeposit box where archaic images are stored. Institutions must make adjust-ments. New styles and labels have emerged in that sensitive barome-ter of change, the arts—not only what we traditionally call "fine" arts, but popular ones as well. Look again at the TV commercials, McDonald's hamburger stands, neon signs, comics, supermarkets, superbowls. Elitists have long called all this the Wasteland; but in the new popstyle mythology, this is the raw material from which new sagas will be constructed.

Some of the visual groundwork has already been laid by a group of Pop Artists. In the 1950's clusters of them started studying pop music, advertising, Hollywood films, cybernetics, auto styling. Their work embodied comic strips, soap operas, merchandise in stores. The world inside and outside the studio were merged. "Painting relates to both art and life," one of the generation's leader, Robert Rauschen-berg, said. "Neither can be ignored. I try to act in the gap between the two."

When the whole man-made environment was a possible subject for art, the whole field was rejuvenated, might this not happen in mythology? Religion is the state of being ultimately concerned. Art symbolizes that concern, transforming it into color, sound, symbol. Religion and art blend in mythology.

The style generated by a highly urban, technical, democratic society, like contemporary America, is popstyle. It serves as a mirror held up to today's American.

The environment of this American is global; he is "into" Oriental politics, African sculpture, prehistoric caves, Zen scriptures, the click-clack of computers. He seeks, like his precursors the surrealists, things as beautiful as the chance encounter of a sewing machine with an umbrella on an operating table.

One key to popstyle is coalescence. Time, space, and tradition have been so wedded that all old barriers are down. Things from "the distant past"— astrology, witchcraft, acupuncture—are as up-to-date as the morning newspaper. Welcome to the eternal Now. All the past is now; so is all the future. Gone forever is the chicken-and-egg argument. The chicken was the egg's idea for getting more eggs.

Gone forever is the country-rhythm, nature-centered world which made folklore and folkstyle central for man. When the literate Greeks abstracted visual order out of oral chaos, they called their artifact "Nature" (*phusis*). But in today's electric world (as Marshall McLuhan points out)[1] man has come to see this "nature" as an extension of himself, just as he is an extension of nature. To this extent, nature itself has dropped out. Where did it go?

"But the melody lingers on." We live in an era of fakelore and fakestyle. One of the first people to perceive this was Walter Lippman. In 1922, when he published *Public Opinion,* he spoke of "the urge to oversimplify patterns." Forty years later, in *The Image: A Guide to Pseudo-Events in America,* Daniel Boorstin analyzed pseudo-events, made more dramatic than mere reality since they are planned with that in mind. Repeatable at will, pseudo-events spawn other such events in geometric fashion. He formulated a new Gresham's law for fakestyle: counterfeit happenings will always drive spontaneous ones out of circulation. Poison tastes so sweet that it spoils one's appetite for plain fact. Those seeking "the unadorned truth" find their subject disappearing under their very eyes.

The flowering of fakestyle, not only in the United States but the Western World, came in the 19th century. Artsycrafty movements, such as those sparked by Ruskin and Morris in England, allowed a whole generation to retreat into a Prince Gallant past.

In their comic opera *Patience*, Gilbert and Sullivan produced a brilliant satire of Victorian fakestyle. The hero, Bunthorne, advises us to "Be eloquent in praise of the very dull old days which have long since passed away." The Duke admits:

> It's clear that mediaeval art alone retains its zest,
> To charm and please its devotees we've done our
> little best.

This is precisely the attitude on which fakestyle rests; it is not built on imagination (like folkstyle) but on imitation. It was a necessary and transitional period between two vigorous and indigenous styles: folk and pop. Poets have long imitated the ballad; pseudo-folktales and epics are not rare. But in the late nineteenth century what Daniel G. Hoffman calls "the dynamics of transmission" altered.[2] New mass media began to manipulate folk opinions and to create a new "climate." An old culture was vanishing; a new one had not yet developed.

Now, in the last generation before the 21st century, fakestyle is being supplanted by popstyle; popular culture is becoming a subject in Universities throughout the world. Dimensions and boundaries are still amorphous. The "Craze to Define" sometimes overcomes the "Urge to Understand." Still it may already be possible to make distinctions and connections between folk-, fake-, popstyles:

FOLKSTYLE	FAKESTYLE	POPSTYLE
oral	verbal	multisensory
traditional	nostalgic	experimental
realistic	romantic	psychedelic
earthy	sticky	tart
homespun	factory-spun	polyester
continuity	transition	explosion
improvised	ersatz	electronic
cowboy	Buffalo Bill	Bonanzaland
community sing	folk festival	Disneyland

The structure of the nuclear family, on which society has rested for centuries, is being challenged by communes—a whole new style of living.[3] Manifestations of radical change emerge in buildings by Robert Venturi, films by Bernardo Bertolucci, essays by Susan Sontag or Tom Wolfe. Writing "On Style," Ms. (which has supplanted "Miss" and "Mrs.") Sontag defines style as the principle of decision in a work of art; the signature of the artist's will. Those signatures—not only in words but images, gestures, sounds point to a Declaration of Independence.

Speaking the new *lingua franca* of popular culture, young Americans are discovering new modes of experience, new ways to achieve depth and involvement. One visible, notable achievement is the musical *Hair*, produced first in 1967 by Joseph Papp. With no fixed text and endless improvization, it provides a new kind of entertainment: a do-it-yourself earth ritual, complete with altar, sacred fire, and litanies. By 1970, *Hair* was playing in 14 countries, with 6 troupes touring the United States. *Jesus Christ, Superstar* and *Godspell* had equally impressive receptions. They demonstrated that any new mythology draws from and transforms old ones. They also showed that to invent myths we must ask questions about being, the logos of reality.

Power plus structure equals a life of being. Those who are young in the 1970's may well after 2000 A.D. look back upon their lives, and echo the famous couplet of William Wordsworth:

> Bliss was it in that day to be alive;
> But to be young was very heaven.

14. GLOBES

The great globe itself . . . shall dissolve.

—Shakespeare

They were like sardines, freshly canned.

Head to head, tail to tail, sealed into place, no ventilation, no place to go.

Their can was a 707 Jet, their shelf the approach runway to Takeoff Lane Number 5 at JFK Airport in New York City. A kind of bogged-down United Nations: India, France, and Japan waiting in a long line ahead; airplanes flagged as Germany, Brazil, and Ethiopia behind.

It was midnight on a July night hot enough for Dante's Inferno. The passengers were dead tired. For weeks they had been reading guidebooks, thumbing through traveller's checks, double-checking passports and yellow health cards. By noon they had been bumper to bumper along the expressways. Check in at six, due out at eight, board plane at ten, taxi out at eleven and then—be a sardine.

The air conditioning wasn't working. The first drink was long down, and regulations prohibited serving another before take-off.

"How many planes in front of us?" a tussled Mother asked the Alitalia stewardess.

"Only a few, Madam," she replied, smiling and trying to look very Italian.

"A few, huh?" said the man looking out the small window, little

beads of perspiration glistening on his cheeks. "Like 12 or 13."
"There might have been an accident," the Stewardess suggested.
"Maybe. Now if you can just arrange a miracle maybe we can go on
to Rome."
Some passengers tried to sleep. Perhaps they dreamed of Rome,
with its dank, gloomy catacombs, mellowed crumbling hills, cool
gushing fountains. Mighty and majestic, sad and dying, parched and
polluted—not just the Eternal City but the Eternal Asylum for anybody from anywhere who wants to run away from home.
Rome, the timeless refugee camp for tourists, pilgrims, saints,
murderers, merchants, scholars, film-makers, hucksters, hippies,
artists. Home-makers, girl-makers, verse-makers, bomb-makers: their
roads converge here. They are the exiles, left with only memories of
the lost Eden, somehow detoured around paradise.
Roma, non basta una vita. One lifetime isn't enough to see Rome.
So I start seeing it—in my mind's eye—from the inside of my swelter-
ing super-sardine can.
April 12, 753 B.C. Rome begins.
And now 1,220 years later, we can't even get this damn plane to
fly to Rome. Progress. Jupiter, Juno, and Minerva, have mercy upon
us.
As we have not had mercy on you. Nothing is more ridiculous
than an old worn-out god or goddess. Pretenders must be hung by
their heels (like Mussolini in Milan) for public display and scorn. Gods
must win, because our blood turns sour and sticky when they loose.
Of course, they may lose their lives and still win. That is why the
pagan Olympus was supplanted by a Christian heaven. With the
martyrdom of Saint Polycarp, the Romans found a formula for veneration that has held Rome together for centuries. When heroes got
haloes, Rome created the greatest tourist attraction of all time.
The landscape there is full of tombs, catacombs, and bones.
Nothing is so sweet as the distant smell of death. Once the flesh has
rotted the clean white bones are the building blocks of idolatry and
mythology. Rome is the boneyard of the classical world.
That same Rome is a generator of the electrified Global Village.
No designers surpass the Italians in clothes, shoes, automobiles, fabrics.

Italian films are startling and superb. In 1972 Italian publishers turned out over 235,000,000 copies of 200 different comic books; the most popular featured "Topolino"—Disney's Mickey Mouse. More important: Italians act out comic book roles, on TV, stage, town square. Italy is full of wonderful actors—but most of them are never on stage.

Events in Italian streets remind me of scenes from vintage Marx Brothers movies . . . like the one in which chaos takes over in a small cabin on a steamer. Plumbers, electricians, manicurists, and cleaners rush about madly: sardines gone berserk inside their can. A lady tries in vain to make a telephone call. Chico, dressed in an army helmet, helps carry in a cot on which Harpo sleeps peacefully. Groucho, meanwhile, concentrates on seducing the manicurist.

Why do we love Rome so? Because it is so old? No—because it is so new. Bread, fruit, films, and waiters are all fresh. The latest plastic toy is as revered as the oldest basilica. Tenors are valued more than prime ministers—and American rock groups more than anything. The Eternal City is Now.

While William Jennings Bryan was pushing free silver in the United States, the Italian Futurists were stressing speed, machines, and motion. Their 1909 *Manifesto* was an early attempt to baptize popular culture; the role of Gino Severini, Umberto Boccioni, Giogio Morandi, and Alberto Savinio has been vastly underestimated.[1] I will want to toast them, looking down on the Roman Forum, swarming with tired tourists and criminal cats. I will ask myself: what is there that makes this past such an unmistakable part of the 20th century? How could the culture that defied Hannibal and the Golden Horde be won by Coca Cola? Why are all these ruins wired for sound? Why do Italian babies fall asleep clutching plastic Mickey Mouses?

Italy: haven for priests, plastics, popular culture. In this she is a spectacular but not a unique example. The Iron Curtain doesn't keep out the popular sounds and images of our times. The same beat to which London swings is heard in Moscow, Cracow, and Budapest. And wait till you hear the way they sing country western music in Tokyo!

This is not a naive statement about the "Brotherhood of Man" or the universality of Love-Ins. Old racial and ethnic struggles continue, aggravated, perhaps, by the verbal and electronic overkill. Plainly the Oldstyle hate-baiting politicians continue to be nationalistic and ethnocentric, but new lifestyles are geocentric and irresistible. Once diplomats and professors represented American life in faraway places; then tourists. In the 1970's students are on the move: they will be everywhere, moving freely across borders and "doing their thing." Life will be ever more multicultural. The idea that a nation, state, department, or community can box others out has always been a short-sighted strategy. Soon it will be simply an impossibility.

Observe our young revolutionaries at work and play. They have borrowed their philosophy from Mao, their rhetoric from Che Guevara, their shock troop tactics from Japanese radicals. The youthquake is global; and it has only begun.

If "popular culture" is the non-elite non-academic culture which excludes no one at the bottom and molds even those at the top who question or scorn it, then an international pop style has emerged in the mid-twentieth century. The old folkstyle is updated and electrified; guitar-players and banjo-pickers are still with us, but their instruments are juiced up-up-up. The television screen has taken the place of the vaudeville stage and the tent show. Thus the term "popular arts," used in the late 19th century, deals with substitutes for or extensions of such traditional arts as drama, poetry, fiction, and painting.[2]

In addition, there are entirely new art forms, such as the cinema, which arose from the popular desire to see pictures move. Nor could Grandfather ever imagine, except in his wildest dream, an Electric Circus.

Not only popular culture, dispensed by mass media, but all art and literature are becoming common property. Travel, interchanges, scholarships, translations, reproductions, and exhibitions on both public and private levels are eliminating old barriers and frontiers. Only a few men have been to the moon; but millions have seen televised views of our small blue bulb spinning in a vast void. Can any one doubt that we have the same address, are part of the same enterprise?

C. P. Snow's "two cultures" dilemma is outmoded. The sharp

line between the arts and sciences is disappearing. Think of words that apply equally well to both: far out, experimental, interface, turned on, dynamic, nebular, freefall, random, fused, amorphous. Except in some universities, medieval walls between traditional disciplines have come tumbling down. One trumpet announcing that fall is popular culture.

The moon landing and skylab is only one illustration of technical progress and globe-shrinking. The recent history of the world abounds with other examples. Battery-powered transistor radios, jet planes, and communications satellites are world-wide commodities. Thousands of years of historical isolation disappeared. Images and ideas were transformed.

Rudyard Kipling notwithstanding, the *twain* has met—East and West swing together. Report after report from Asia (especially Japan) tell of "spurting sales of electric guitars, pop records, and comic books." Our music, simultaneously, reflects an ever-growing Eastern influence, as does the lifestyle of our young. In the spring of 1973, the New York *Times* reported, large numbers of them flocked to Kabul in Afghanistan:

> They were called hippies just a few years ago
> but now—perhaps because the phrase sounds
> more quixotic, romantic—the young Europeans
> and Americans define themselves as simply
> world travelers.[3]

In another part of the world, Leonid I. Brezhnev, Soviet leader, was travelling to the west, via East Germany. The Communist Party there marshaled thousands of young people to welcome him; Hedrick Smith, a New York *Times* reporter, was on hand. "They were toting guitars and sporting hip-hugging, bell-bottomed slacks and stringy unisex hair," he wrote. "Groups entertained themselves with Western folk rock. One blue-jacketed ensemble had even worked out a rock-beat propaganda tune with a rhythmic refrain of "Solidarität—Ooh—Ah—Ah."

Speaking of Europe, our plane has inched forward, and we are about to shoot out over the Atlantic. "Globes make my head spin," a student said recently. "By the time I locate a place, the boundaries are changed." Which boundaries, borders, parameters will hold?

We are off. Sardines of the world, unite! You have nothing to lose but your cans!

15. TWO WALTS

O brave new world!

—Shakespeare

Here's our problem: people who have style tend not to write about it; and people who write about style usually don't have much.

Style: a characteristic mode, manner, or method of expression; excellence, skill, or grace in performance, manner or appearance. It. Umph. Zing. . . .

The term style gets attached to almost everything: cultures, nations, dynasties, artists, periods, crafts. The literature of art twists through the labyrinthine network of the notion of style. Despite its constant use—and misuse—the word style remains a mystery. What brings a dead object to life is hidden within the viewer, not the object; but what turns a person, or a nation, on?

"When you have described a civilization's people, armies, technology, economics, arts class, caste, mores, and morals," Max Lerner writes in *America as a Civilization*, "there is something else . . . an inner civilization style."

Is there in fact such an "inner style"? Depending on where "it" begins, who first exemplified it—Cotton Mather, William Byrd, Benjamin Franklin, Thomas Jefferson, Eli Whitney? Or Henry Thoreau, who refused to count the cats in Zanzibar? Or—?

Inevitably we end up agreeing with Peter and Linda Murray: "The proper practice of stylistic analysis is more difficult than it

116

sometimes seems to be."[1]

No matter how difficult, we must deal with style if we would know the parameters of popular culture. Style has to do with formulae and model-building; it is not something that determines the creative process, but which is a result of that process.[2] Alexis de Tocqueville realized this as early as 1825. He assumed that from America's "motley multitude," her "heterogeneous and agitated," a new nation and a new style would surely arise. That there is a powerful American nation no one can doubt. Is there an American style?

Few questions have been asked so often and answered so indecisively. Whole volumes—like Elting Morison's collection on *The National Style* (New York, 1960)—have appeared. Even before the nation was formed, enlightened patriots like Thomas Jefferson and Benjamin Franklin wrote constantly about what was and was not "American." "After the first cares for the necessaries of life are over," Franklin wrote to a European friend in 1780, "we shall come to think of the embellishments. Already some of our young geniuses begin to lisp attempts at painting, poetry, and music." That opens the door to minute studies of the lispers. Jefferson, who liked to collect his own information, collected moose antlers to refute the charge of French naturalist Buffon that animals "deteriorated" in the New World. Jefferson's *Notes on Virginia* remain a model for documenting exactly what one portion of America is like, according to 18th century cosmology.

My brief comments on "Ameristyle" will involve no long chronological analysis; no search for new branches and old roots. That has been done—and will be done many more times. I prefer to present a modest parable—the Tale of Two Walts.

Walt Whitman, a carpenter's son, was born on a Long Island farm in 1819. Like Henry Thoreau, he was an authentic nativist who never went abroad. A restless and explosive young man, Walt drifted into the city and joined the staff of the crusading Brooklyn *Eagle*. The noisy pushy world of news reporters, scoops, and headlines fascinated the farm boy; from the first he kept scrapbooks of clippings to shove later into his poems. "Be simple and clear—be not occult" Whitman wrote in his "Notebook" during 1848. That single sentence comes as close to defining Ameristyle as any ever written.

He talked, travelled, and mixed Beowulf, Broadway, and the Bible to make his own literary concoctions. Gradually Whitman perfected a new style and rhythm; he became "a man standing in the open air." With a directness and honesty that is too daring to be merely conceited, he announced he was his own chief subject. His first "Inscription" began:

> One's -self I sing, a simple separate person,
> Yet utter the word Democratic, the world En-Masse.
> Yes, he would sing. It would be a "Song of Myself":
> I celebrate myself, and sing myself,
> And what I assume you shall assume,
> For every atom belonging to me as good belongs to
> > you.
> I loafe and invite my soul,
> I lean and loafe at my ease observing a spear of sum-
> mer grass.

There's a lot of leaning and loafing in Ameristyle—people as different as Daniel Boone, Abraham Lincoln, Gary Cooper, and Flip Wilson come quickly to mind. But don't be deceived. These people are not relaxed. They are compressed coiled springs ready to spring. They are all superbly self-assured. In Whitman's words:

> I breathe the fragrance myself and know it and
> > like it,
> The distillation would intoxicate me also, but I
> > shall not let it.

The question is, how did this untrained and uncritical writer find a harmony to balance his contradictions? How did he develop a style that matched perfectly what he wanted and needed to say?

"I was simmering and Emerson brought me to a boil," Whitman admitted; but Emerson writes more like a cranky European stylist than an open-road man. Whitman himself drew from various European forms and canons—dream visions, sagas, German mystical thought, for example—but he was a great and original craftsman. He developed an elaborate and complicated system of special devices (repetition, hovering accents, and caesuras) and lied when he claimed "I have never given any study to mere expression." Like Mark Twain and Ernest Hemingway, he cultivated his uncouthness.

His style was so new, so unorthodox, that no one wanted to print his collected poems called *Leaves of Grass*. So Whitman set up, printed, and distributed the book himself. Ameristyle dates from that book, that year (1855). The opening inscriptions made it clear what was to be encompassed—physiology from top to toe; a simple separate person; the passion, pulse, and power of Modern Man. "I know perfectly well my own egotism," Whitman admitted with disarming frankness, "Know my omnivorous lines and must not write any less." He described dirt farmers, prostitutes, Negroes, the body electric, city of orgies, ganders that say *Ya-honk* in the cool night. There had never been a book like this, full of barbaric yawps that itched the ears. The genteel poets shuddered. Lowell found Whitman "as unacquainted with art as a hog is with mathematics." The Boston Intelligencer found neither wit nor method in his "disjointed babbling." Whittier could say nothing—he quickly burned his copy of *Leaves of Grass*.

A century later we recognize in Walt Whitman one of the authentic voices of his day and the New World. The word that best summarizes him is *fluid*. Words, thoughts, phrases, ideas flow, expressing an inexhaustible interest and faith in the world around him. As his critics point out, there are few good lines in his poems. He didn't write them to be dissected, line by line, and analyzed. They must be *felt*, being more visceral than intellectual. He draws the reader into the poem, intriguing him with specific details, but revealing finally a world floating in space. "Crossing Brooklyn Ferry," my favorite poem, catches the very moment of suspension, at twilight, when the sea gull glides effortlessly on the wind. The world is soft and lovely. Whitman accepts it completely, and makes us accept it too.

New ideas fascinated him. "I accept evolution from A to Izzard," he announced. The wildness of the jungle—both nature-made and man-made—was a subject of never-ending interest. "I am not a bit tamed," he bragged. "I too am untranslatable." So he fished, shouted poetry at the sea, went west, rode with Old Peter on the Broadway horsecar, nursed Civil War soldiers (Johnny Reb, Billy Yank, white, black, all shades in between), kept travelling the open road. His unique mixture of the concrete and abstract, vast scope and breadth, and blatant contradictions all pointed towards the twentieth century. The poetry he left is so teeming with the potencies of life that we encounter not so much a book as a man. His foothold, he wrote, was "tenon'd and mortis'd in granite"—a sturdy foundation on which Pop Culture might build.

Whitman had been dead six years when in 1899 Walter Elias Disney was born in Chicago. Like Whitman, he was a maverick and a wanderer. Still in his teens during World War I, Disney went to France and drove an ambulance. Returning to America, he took art lessons and drew sketches for farm magazines. Then he became interested in animated cartoons, and made a series in Kansas City. Walt's first animal was Oswald the Rabbit, a descendant of B'rer Rabbit and Uncle Remus. Oswald was moderately successful but when the distributor refused an advance Walt resigned and headed west for Hollywood. En route a Mouse was born.[3]

And what a mouse: Everyman, Renaissance, and Superman rolled into one; at different times a pioneer, hunter, detective, lover, tailor, and athlete. Because his promulgators were so sensitized to popular tastes, heroes, and trends, Mickey Mouse was for a whole generation a prefabricated barometer of popular culture.[4] He was wholly, but not merely, American. More people knew him as Michel Souris, Miguel Ratonocito, Miki Kuchi, Mikki Hirri, Musse Pigg, and Mikel Mus than as Mickey Mouse.

Indeed, folklore has always contained a spot for mouselore. Old folk traditions tell of a magic mouse skin, micely transformations, and city-country mice feuds. Tales of mice stronger than mountains, braver than lions, abound.[5] Once a mouse put his tail in a sleeping thief's mouth and made him cough up a magic ring. A sassy mouse taunted a ferocious bull. Other mice devoured a bad bishop in a tower still visible from the Rhine River.

There is no indication that Disney was a student of mouselore; but like the earlier Walt, he had a wonderful feeling for the American idiom, the gusty spirit, and things that attracted ordinary people. Both Walts were, in their own way, rebels against elite culture.

They also shared a strong streak of sentimentality. The saga of Mickey Mouse draws from the Horatio Alger success myth. With pluck and luck our underdog hero comes through and foils more powerful and arrogant adversaries. Disney's stories are morality plays, reduced to a lowest common denominator.

Technologically, however, they are sophisticated and innovative. It takes 16 drawings to make Mickey move once on the screen. A ten-minute cartoon requires 14,400 pictures, carefully synchronized with the sound tracks by a process called "Mickey Mousing." In the McLuhan sense, Mickey is a cool hero—not well defined, leaving much to the visual imagination of viewers. That is why a real-life photograph (which is very hot) is an intrusion into the world of animated cartoons.

Observe the ever-popular Mickey in his various roles. He tackles the machine, which might be a vacuum cleaner, meat grinder, or cement mixer. If he is the symbolic foil of Frankenstein, the machined man, he is totally unlike the Monster physically. Franken-stein is big, unwieldy, humorless, destructive; Mickey is tiny, agile, funny, compassionate. Those of us who find the modern world intimidating and sometimes overwhelming can empathize with Mickey; he fights his battles (like Charlie Chaplin) for the little guys. Cast in the Aesop genre, Mickey is a moralist. Like characters in any memorable drama he distorts to make real. Mickey oversimplifies to make his points. His Pop World has a logic of its own and he achieves an illusion of independence from his technocrat-creators.

The success of Disney's later enterprises (nature films, True-Life Adventures, Donald Duck's series, safety films, man-in-space series, etc.) need not be detailed here. In various experiments he did not hesitate to mix media and even genres. In one cartoon, for example, he had the drawing board Donald Duck pursue a flesh-and blood chorus girl: a spectacle bizarre enough to bring a Society to Keep Live Actors Out of Disney Movies into being. What his critics fail to notice is that Disney was King of Camp long before Susan Sontag brought the word into vogue. Why else would a market-wise producer confront the tough existential world of the 1960's with a full-length "straight" production of *Pollyanna* and make a pile of money for his efforts? (In 1962 the Disney studios had a gross income of nearly $75,000,000.)

If Pop Culture has a slogan, it is: "You're putting me on." Existentially free from the moralism and negativism which plagued the 1940's and 1950's, the new era not only accepts the new technology, but pokes fun at it. Instead of rejection we have exaltation. The operative word is *magic*. This is the feeling thousands of visitors have gotten from visiting Disneyland, that "magic kingdom" opened in 1955 near Anaheim, California. Robert de Roos captures the flavor in his article on "The Magic Worlds of Walt Disney":

> Audio-Animatronic figures are now being plan-
> ned for Disneyland's French Quarter square in
> old New Orleans. They will also add chilling
> realism to the Haunted Mansion now under con-
> struction in Frontierland. (Visitors are told,
> "Walt's out capturing ghosts for it now.")[6]

This streak of romanticism, and penchant for the occult, is a quality shared by our two Walts. Do you remember these three Whitman people, conjured up in *Salut au Monde*:

> You sheiks along the stretch from Suez to
>   Bab-el-mandeb ruling your families and tribes!
> You olive-growing tending your fruit on fields of
>   Nazareth, Damascus, or lake Tiberias!
> You Thibet trader on the wide inland or bargaining
>   in the shops of Lassa!

Despite differences in technique and temperament, Whitman and Disney had much in common. They were both obsessed with detail, versimilitude, vulgarity, and innovation. What other poets would describe his body as in *Children of Adam*:

> Head, neck, hair, ears, drop and tympan of the
> ears,
> Eyes, eye-fringes, iris of the eye, eyebrows, and
> the waking or sleeping
> of the lids,
> Mouth, tongue, lips, teeth, roof of the mouth,
> jaws, and the jaw-hinges. . . .

And on and on, coming finally to the heel; then doubling back to pick up love-looks, love-perturbations, freckles, and

> The curious sympathy one feels when feeling
> with the hand the naked
> meat of the body.

Here is that combination of objectivity, versimilitude, and vulgarity that one feels as he walks around Disneyland (alias Cornsville, U.S.A.) with its *ersatz* Emporium, flying elephants in Fantasyland, clay *Tyrannosaurus rex* with a two-foot mouthful of six-inch teeth, and a plastic baby elephant which entertains "Jungle Cruise Voyagers" by squirting water into the jaws of a crocodile.

As for impressive detailed listings of Disney doings, one need only inquire about the equipment (telescopic lenses, zoom lenses, time-lapse cameras, synchronized cameras, underwater cameras, etc.) used by Disney's cameramen-naturalists who spent months in primitive areas, African heat, Alaskan blizzards, and South American jungles to achieve the authenticity Disney craved.

In this way, with these obsessions, both Walts prepared us for the extension of their attitudes in Pop art, in the work of Claes Oldenberg, Donald Judd, Robert Rauschenberg, Roy Lichtenstein, Burgoyne Diller, Kenneth Noland, and many others.

Another similarity between our two Walts is their fascination with Abraham Lincoln. Whitman's two best known poems ("O

Captain, My Captain," and "When Lilacs Last in the Dooryard Bloom'd") laud the martyred hero. A century later Disney's technicians made an Audio-Animatronic Lincoln, who not only looked and moved like the real man, but could (with the help of an electronic console) explain to visitors: "Our reliance is in the love of liberty which God has planted in us. . . ."

Here, in Disneyland, is Popstyle Abe: with 16 air lines to his head, 10 to his hands and wrists, 14 hydraulic lines to control his body, and two pairs of wires for every line. Electronic Age can not only raise each eyebrow quizzically, nod, and fix you with a glance— he can even put you at ease with a genial wink.

From one Walt, instant poetry; from the other, instant character. In both, the unmistakable American ring.

The critical question with the two Walts, and the popstyle they pioneered, is "Can we take them seriously?" Is this bumptious fellow who shouts "the glory and wonder of body electric" a true poet, and this creator of Silly Symphonies an artist? Yes—we not only can but must take both Walts seriously.

Scorning the "high seriousness" of the academy and the pulpit, they were undiscouraged believers in the essential goodness of human nature, and their own power to express it in the American idiom. Europeans like Sean O'Casey have recognized this:

> Walt Whitman, one of the world's good wishes
> Is the one that wishes you here.
> To sing, shake hands to the world's peoples
> To listen, cock-ear'd, in a way of wonder,
> To all the others have got to say. . . .

Few critics, elite or popular, have had such kind words for Walt Disney. Never mind. If not his soul, then at least his kingdom, goes marching on. His giant stake-out in mid-Florida, Disney World, is fast becoming what the bumper stickers claim: "Vacationland for the World." With admirable Yankee ingenuity and adaptability, those who carry on Walt's work without his presence, have invented The Orange Bird, "communicating through the puffs of orange smoke which carry his thoughts." Since making his appearance on "The Walt Disney World Grand Opening TV Special" in 1972, The Bird "is seen daily in the Florida Citrus Sunshine Pavillion." Advertising gives way to fantasizing; substance to shadows. The package becomes the product. Alice, try *that* for a Wonderland!

16. TWO WARS

I won't be reconstructed
And I just don't give a damn.

—Southern Folk Song

Have you served in the army?
No, I have seen the army on TV.

—Jerzy Kosinski, *Being
There* (1972)

Long before Rhett Butler told Scarlett O'Hara that frankly he
didn't give a damn, the Civil War had a special spot in the American
imagination. It was a cause, a cult, a spectacle, and (if you were a
Southerner) an explanation for everything that was wrong with contemporary America.

When I was a boy in Virginia, there were still a few old veterans
walking around—hobbling would be better, for those I knew had lost
a leg. They were, of course, demigods. To a man they had been with
Lee at Gettysburg and had surrendered the last battle flag at Appomattox. Respect was their due; youthful awe their reward. They
went gently back into the green fields they had once defended.

Naturally, I learned early that what Yankees called the Civil
War was The War between the States—though Lost Cause was all right
to other Southerners. "Rebel" was an honorable, a glorious word.
Who could doubt it, seeing those marble soldiers guarding every court

house and town square in Dixie?

That "the War" (others followed—but this was *the* War) fascinated Yankees as well as Rebels could be confirmed by best-seller lists or movie guides. Civil War fans increased by geometrical progressions and young recruits filled the ranks of the "buffs." "A tacit agreement exists between War authors, readers, and reviewers," historian Frank E. Vandiver noted in 1959. "They will not double-cross each other by questioning the virtue of anything written about 'the War.' The subject has a special sanctity conferred by popularity. If it's about the Civil War, it's got to be good!"[1]

I had to grow up, fight another war, and study at a university in the Yankee heartland (Yale) before I realized that there were not one but two Civil Wars; before I understood why (according to Plutarch) Pyrrhus used to say that Cineas had taken more towns with his words than he had with his arms.

Civil War I, a military affair, was fought with blood, guts, and shrapnel; it left us the vision of Cold Harbor and Appomattox. Civil War II is part of popular culture and is waged with print, films, and P. R. men. Book lists and film festivals confirm the report from the battle front: the Yankees are everywhere in retreat. Page by page, film by film, the neo-Confederates are sweeping the field.[2]

Civil War I heroes are well remembered. Transported to the Confederate Valhalla, their memories and mementoes are guarded by the Vestal Virgins of the United Daughters of the Confederacy. Able historians have told their stories; many Southern universities are still at it. They have begun to smack of the mythological.

Let me call attention to four little-known writers and a photographer who set the stage for Civil War II. Their words and images formed a causeway between a bloody realistic war and a euphoric romantic one. My contention is not only that their work helps to explain the incredible and unfading popularity of the Civil War; but that it also indicates the type of research students of popular culture must do in other areas if they want to give factual substance to their theories. Look at George William Bagby, John Esten Cooke, Thomas Nelson Page, John Tabb, and Michael Miley.

George William Bagby managed to sleep through the Battle of

Bull Run. Once awakened, he fought and viewed a lot. He saw
Virginia under fire and eventually under heel. Watching the new day
come he never forgot the old. His vindication came not by the
ephemeral sword but by the enduring word.

Born on a Buckingham County plantation in 1828 Bagby volun-
teered for the Confederate army but was eventually discharged on
account of ill health. He edited the *Southern Literary Messenger* before purchasing *The Native Virginian*. As a writer he had a mission
"to describe everything distinctive and without parallel in Virginian
civilization, which culminated in the war and perished at its close."
Bagby's best sketch was *The Old Virginia Gentleman*. "There was in
our Virginia country life a beauty, a simplicity, a purity, an upright-
ness, a cordial and lavish hospitality, warmth, and grace which shine
in the lens of memory with a charm that passes all language at command," Bagby claimed. "It is gone with the social structure that
gave it birth." Despite such romantic nostalgia, Bagby was essentially
a realist in his descriptions and attitudes. He marveled that so
chivalrous a group of peers as those described in Civil War novels
could have produced so many scoundrels as he saw about him in his
lifetime. He had a sharpness of vision that made his work fascinating
to a twentieth-century writer like Ellen Glasgow. "His sketches have
always been a part of my Virginia heritage," she wrote. "The vital
warmth and humanity of the writing give him a permanent place in
the literature of Virginia."

Yet there is no satire in Bagby's poem about General Lee called
"After Appomattox." It was as though in the rear of Lee's tent had
been the Ark of the Covenant. Like most Virginians, Bagby simply
stood in awe of the Great Leader, as he imagines Lee on his knees
just after the surrender to Grant:

> The cries that upward went that night
> Unto the great White Throne,
> The tears for guidance and for light
> To God alone are known.
>
> Sacred throughout all coming time

These sleepless hours shall be;
For who can tell in words sublime
The agony of Lee?

If he couldn't tell, John Esten Cooke was at least willing to try.
Born in northern Virginia and admitted to the bar in 1851, Cooke
was an eager gentleman-novelist. His aim was "to paint the Virginia
phase of American society, to do for the Old Dominion what Cooper
has done for the Indians, Simms for the Revolutionary drama in
South Carolina, Irving for the Dutch Knickerbockers, and Hawthorne
for the Puritan life of New England." In 1854 Cooke wrote *Leather
Stocking and Silk* and *The Virginia Comedians.* Then followed *Ellie;
or the Human Comedy, The Last of the Foresters,* and *Henry St.
John, Gentleman.* These books showed what the Southern aristocrat
was like and how he lived. The war gave Cooke the chance to find
out, in addition, how he behaved in battle.

An ardent secessionist, he turned all the Confederate generals
(including the Calvinistic Jackson) into cavalier knights. Somehow,
between battles in which he participated, Cooke managed to write
The Life of Stonewall Jackson (1863). Enemy forces never interfered
with his literary chores or his meals. Continuing to eat from a plate
near his horse until the Yankees were within two hundred yards, he
would gulp down his coffee and gallop away. Southern readers warmed
to an author who scribbled in his diary: "I tried to write in a tent, on
the outpost; the enemy yonder, almost on us—but with Jackson, alas,
no longer in front. Oh, to write in a quiet study, with no enemy anywhere in view."

Cooke hurried home from Appomattox, where he buried his
spurs as a last act of defiance, to write Civil War novels. *Surry of
Eagle's Nest* (1866) and *Mohun* (1869) show the romantic possibilities
of Civil War fiction. Cooke, whose long point was not plotting or
organizing, frequently stopped his story to throw in documentary
information. Thus *Mohun* contains one of our best descriptions of
Richmond just before its fall. In his latter years, William Dean Howells
and other writers were popularizing a type of realism which was
antithetical to Cooke's work; but it did not bother him. "I was born

too soon, and am now too old to learn my trade anew," he said. He kept writing, and the people kept reading what he wrote. Many of them still do. He was a cavalier romancer to the end.

Younger and more talented than Bagby or Cooke was Thomas Nelson Page in whose veins ran some of Virginia's best blood. Two of his great-grandfathers had been governors. His father served on General Lee's staff. Only twelve when the war ended, Thomas saw the old regime in his most impressionable years and idealized it all the rest of his life. At Washington College he knew and revered General Lee. Brilliant and personable, Page turned his talents to literature and gave the phrase "before the war" a special meaning. Borrowing from Russell, Cable, and Harris, he pioneered in local-color writing, working out a literary formula which captured the North as well as the South. This is how it went:

> Take a white-haired ex-slave, yearning for "de best days Sam eber see." Have him describe the plantation Eden, stressing the justice and juleps of Old Marse, the dash and swagger of Young Marse, and the sweet perfection of Southern ladies. Throw in a few barbecues, christenings, and Christmas feasts.
>
> Then—de wah.
>
> Out with the trumpet and the Confederate flag! Off go Old Marse, Young Marse, and all Marses in the neighborhood to lead an army of gentlemen and poor whites to daring victory against incredible odds. Young Marse dies on the field of honor. Now only Sam, young Marse's faithful dog, and a Lady-Who-Will-Never-Tell keep alive his gallant memory.

Page wrote novels, short stories, and poems using the format. A typical example is "Uncle Gabe's White Folks," which appeared in *Scribner's Monthly* in 1876:

'Fine old place?' Yes suh, 'tis so
An' mighty fine people my white folks war—
But you ought ter a' seen it years ago
When de Marster an' de Missus lived up dyah;
When de nigger'd stan' all roun' de do'
Like grains o' corn on the cornhouse flo'.

Page's poems found a national audience by extolling the virtues
of slavery, which the United States had spent four agonizing years
destroying, and of reconciliation to the new freedom. To this end
he developed the "blood will tell" formula. The refined Yankee
soldier saved the refined and defenseless Southern lady from Yankee
scum. After the war he comes back, weds the girl, saves the homestead, and bridges the bloody chasm. Or else (as in *Two Little Con-
federates*) the well-bred Southerners befriend the dying Yankee of
good stock. After the war the Yank's folks repay the debt by saving
the old homestead. Better than anybody else, he expressed the spirit
of the Old South in a way which captivated the New.

Unquestionably Page was sincere in believing that his picture
was accurate and fair. "In the simple plantation homes was a life
more beautiful and charming than any that the gorgeous palaces
would reveal," he insisted. "Its best presentation was that which had
the divine beauty of truth." His books are Virginian to the core. For
him, character is determined by status. Heroic characters are gentlemen; villians are outside the charmed circle.

In Ole Virginia (1887) is pre-eminently the Virginia classic. Anyone who wants to understand the working of the Virginia mind and
the persistence of certain attitudes into the twentieth century should
read it. *The Old Gentleman of the Black Stock, Befo' de War,* and
Marse Chan are other favorites of Page devotees. Mark Twain poked
fun at the formula by having a Negro woman reply to a Yankee's
praise of the Southern moon: "Ah, bless yo' heart, honey, you jes'
ought to seen dat moon befo' de wah!" In *Red Rock,* Page gave his
reply: "For those who knew Virginia as it was then, and can contrast
it with what it has become since, no wonder it seems that even the
moonlight was richer and mellower 'before the war' than it is now."

Page's golden memories appeared in the Brown Decades. Apparently Grant's cohorts, having captured Richmond, were determined to take over the Washington mint as well. The greedy, lawless, and capable coupled startling audacity with immense wastefulness. Leaders of the day, as Vernon Parrington has pointed out, fought their way encased in rhinoceros hides. They had stout nippers. Jim Fisk, for example, bragged that he worshipped in the synagogue of the libertines and when he failed in his Erie Railroad stock swindle he announced cheerfully that nothing had been lost save honor.

Southerners looked back to the happy plantation days with wistful eyes. They turned from the prosaic daily world to the fiction of Thomas Nelson Page. His stories rang true. "Write what you know about," he advised his nephew. "Write as you feel; write simply, clearly, sincerely, and you will write strongly." This is why, far into the twentieth century, the ghost of Page still haunted Southern writers, keening in Negro dialect over Virginia's fallen glories. Through his prose shone the patriarchal glow of days that never will return.

Not all those who made the transition after the war were concerned primarily with defending Old Marse. Among the important if lesser known ex-soldiers were two veterans of Civil War I and of Yankee prison camps, John Tabb and Michael Miley. Both illuminated the period in which they lived, leaving artistic reminders of what they had seen and done.

Born in 1845 on an Amelia County plantation, John Tabb served on a Confederate steamer which made twenty successful runs through the Federal blockade. Finally the ship was captured and the crew sent to the Union prison at Point Lookout, Maryland. There, Tabb met Sidney Lanier, whose friendship was one of the chief pleasures of his life. Released in 1865, Tabb studied for the Episcopal ministry; in 1872 he joined the Roman Catholic Church, a faith which he held for the rest of his life.

"Why don't you come back into the Episcopal Church, John, where you belong?" a friend asked.

"I'll be damned if I do!" Tabb replied.

The young convert taught at St. Charles College (near Ellicott

City, Maryland) until 1881. Ordained a priest in 1884, he spent the remainder of his life at St. Charles College. Several summers he visited and preached in Virginia. Father Tabb was noted for his wit and epigrammatical flare. His own English grammar text was dedicated "To my Pupils, Active and Passive, Perfect and Imperfect, Past, Present, and Future."

Despite lack of recognition and an encroaching blindness, Tabb created delicate and beautiful poems, cameolike in their perfection. Primarily a poet of nature, he drew from his memories of Virginia fields, hills, streams, and clouds. Tabb combined the natural with the scriptural, though his was never a consciously intellectual poetry. "I always see in flashes," he wrote, "and rarely change the first draft of a poem."

Tabb explained the rejection slips he received from *Harper's* and *Scribner's* by admitting that he was a Southern rebel, "and a thoroughly unreconstructed one." The attack of Northern critics on Virginia's Edgar Allan Poe angered him. In 1850, when Tabb was a boy of five, Poe published in *Sartain's Union Magazine* his essay "The Poetic Principle." He defined poetry as the rhythmical creation of beauty and denied that a long poem could exist. In claiming that the "ultimate, perhaps, if we except the dramatic, the only authentic, art form is the lyric," Tabb reflected the views of Poe. He wrote six poems in praise of his master who he thought had found the true poetic principles.

Michael Miley's life, problems, and achievements paralleled Tabb's. Though Tabb was a "Tuckahoe" and Miley a "Cohee," they fought similar battles in both Civil Wars. Tabb left his enduring images on paper; Miley transmitted his to glass plates.

Miley was raised on a Shenandoah Valley farm and educated at the hearth. Only nineteen when he joined the Stonewall Brigade, he was captured at Chancellorsville the day Jackson was shot. Weighing less than a hundred pounds when he was released, Miley returned to the Valley, found his home destroyed, and decided to become a photographer. After a few lessons from an itinerant artisan, he went to Lexington. The magnet that drew him was General Lee and the opportunity of becoming the General's semiofficial photographer.

The series of Lee photographs which he took between 1866 and 1870 is a major addition to the American archives.

Fascinated by Virginia's past, Miley devoted days to copying daguerreotypes of early pioneers, officials, judges, and preachers. He captured on glass many phases of Southern small-town life during Reconstruction. He turned his lens on the village fool and the Negro quarters. Eventually he had fifteen thousand glass plates.

Miley's landscapes are full of spirituality and hope, pointing towards a new art with its own language and idiom. Hemmed in by the Blue Ridge and Allegheny Mountains, which he called "the central feature of our whole life here," he was aware of their overwhelming power, majesty, and timelessness. Miley's camera was no mere machine, but an instrument sensitive to things he could not verbalize. In his best work, Miley combined the two main streams of photography —the utilitarian and the aesthetic.

Michael Miley pioneered in color photography, receiving a patent for his color process on October 21, 1902. Ben Cable, New York businessman and former chairman of the Democratic party, was so impressed that he offered to finance Miley's work if he would come north. Miley declined. His prints could not be mass-produced and sold commercially; not wanting his name associated with inferior craftsmanship, he stayed in the Valley. His untiring experimentation and modifications are documented by hundreds of scrawled notations on the back of unsuccessful or damaged proofs. In these minute scribblings can be read the tedious evolution of his process and the unending quest for a more vivid and flexible medium.

There was no photographer present in 1918 to record Miley's funeral rites, as he had done General Lee's a half-century earlier. The Miley Studio remained open until 1935, when his son Henry sold the whole collection of negatives to the Virginia Historical Society. Like John Tabb and all the other Southern soldiers, Michael Miley rests now in a grave marked with a small iron Confederate cross. On it are two words: *Deo Vindice.*

Not to the obscure grave of Michael Miley, or others whose pioneering work we have mentioned, do tourists go today. They flock to Gettysburg National Park, which had 2,000,000 annual visitors in

1964, double that number in 1970, and where officials estimate the number will double again by 1976.[3]

There is no better place to see Civil War I confront Civil War II than at Gettysburg, where Lee confronted McClellan. John S. Patterson has studied this confrontation in detail, and reported his findings in *Zapped at the Map: The Battlefield at Gettysburg*. At the gates of that battlefield, the 19th century landscape confronts 20th century technology and popular culture: meadow meets amusement park, patriotism intersects with pleasure, free enterprise faces government regulation.

"The two sides of the highway present so many striking contrasts that they often seem altogether distinct; yet one side complements the other, and the two, viewed together, provide an instructive glimpse of American popular culture."

Just so. The popularity of both Civil Wars is no passing thing. It is in the American grain.

17. BUTTONS

Throughout American history, eaters have had it over thinkers. Few first rate logicians, systematic theologians, or metaphysicians have emerged; but of good food and frolic there has been no end. If one fails to extend the parameters of popular culture to the kitchen and the bar, he deserves to be sent off hungry and thirsty. Buttons, too, have popped.

Not all visitors have appreciated America's food cult. Consider that distinguished Englishman, George W. Fatherstonehugh, F.R.S., F. G. S., who visited the fashionable White Sulphur Springs in antebellum Virginia. At dinner the heated subject of conversation, he noted, was Bacon. "How admirable," he remarked, that you care so much about a British philosopher." But he was wrong. They were discussing the hindquarters of a hog.

Even back then, Americans had a long tradition of ample eating. The subject is vast and diverse as the land itself; here I shall speak only of my own corner of it, Virginia. "We have plenty of variety of provisions," the historian Robert Beverly wrote in 1705. "The gentry pretend to have their victuals drest and served up as nicely as if they were in London." Some of their popular favorites were described in what I take to be this country's first published cook book: *The Com-*

pleat Housewife, or Accomplish'd Gentlewoman's Companion (1748). By then Virginia's Governor Alexander Spotswood had staged one of the all-time great "For Men Only" outings in connection with a trek to the top of the Blue Ridge. Though the country gentlemen along complained because "they had no good beds to lie on," they perked up immediately when they stood a-tiptoe on the crest of the mountains and drank a toast to King George. Lieutenant John Fontaine, who kept the official diary, reported:

> We drank the King's health in champagne, and
> fired a volley; the Princess in Burgandy, and
> fired a volley; all the rest in claret, and fired a
> volley. We drank the Governor's health, and
> fired yet another volley.

All this was possible because the Knights of the Golden Horseshoe had included in their provisions "several sorts of liquor, viz.: red wine and white wine, Irish usquebaugh, brandy shrub, two sorts of rum, champagne, canary, cherry punch, cider, etc. etc." One surmises that the explorers were prepared to float the Shenandoah Valley into the British empire.

Gradually America acquired a full-blown mythology with food and drink to sustain it. Man cannot live by bread alone; nor can he divorce that bread from all other aspects of his life. People always live by the mythology of their time. The medievalists had their saints, the *philosophes* their reason, the British their empire. The South had its plantation. Here the alluring Garden of Eden myth found a local habitation and a name. Rural life (to quote Francis P. Gaines' *The Southern Plantation*) was "less hurried, less prosaically equalitarian, less futile, richer in picturesqueness, in realized pleasure that recked not of hope or fear or unrejoicing labor." And full of good things to eat and drink.

Popular novels as well as diaries of the time give detailed accounts of the country gentleman at the table. A memorable example is chapter 33 of John Pendleton Kennedy's *Swallow Barn*, that archetypal novel in which the streams of charm and verisimilitude merged in a broad meadow of episode. Swallow Barn was the name of a fictional plantation—an old edifice which sat like a brooding hen on a riverbank. It was not merely a conglomeration of sticks and stones, but a storehouse of memory and tradition. The great dinner table seemed to be laden not in relationship to the guests' capacity but its own dimensions. At the head, in the customary pride of place, was a goodly ham, rich in its own perfections, as well as the endemic honors that belong to it. On it the cook had carved fanciful figures. Opposite was a huge roasted saddle of mutton which seemed, from its trim and spruce air, ready to gallop off the dish. In between were an enticing diversity of poultry, including fried chicken, sworn brother to the ham, another "must" for every country gentleman's table. Well seasoned, rolled in flour, and sizzled in hot lard, this unjointed fowl was a regional triumph. So were the hot biscuits; a mixture of flour, lard, soda and buttermilk, lightly kneaded, rolled, cut out, baked in an oven till brown, and served piping hot.

Elsewhere on the table interspersed between oysters, crabs, and fish were "a profusion of the products of the garden." Devoted to their vegetables, Southerners have never hesitated to mix them: string or butter beans with corn, peas with rice, okra with tomatoes. They praise the flavor of the so-called "wild greens"—dandelion, pigweed, cowslip, turnip tops. Cooks perfected their own way of seasoning, and passed the secret on to their children. Meanwhile everyone involved ate and ate and ate.

But the last, and perhaps most enduring, mealtime memories were of wine. Writes Kennedy in *Swallow Barn*:

> The courses disappeared; a rich dessert came and
> went; the spirits of the company rose still higher.
> . . . Before us glittered the dark sea of the table,
> studded over with 'carracks,' 'argosies,' and 'barks,'
> freighted with the wealth of the Azores, Spain,
> Portugal and France. In sooth, the wine was very
> good.

The rooms in which these sumptuous banquets occurred were

as impressive as the food. John Esten Cooke included a description in his saga of Squire Effingham, *The Virginia Comedians.* In the outer hall the walls were covered with deer's antlers and guns, family portraits, and pictures of thoroughbred horses. The elegant dining room had a carved oak wainscot extending above the mantlepiece in an unbroken expanse of fruits and flowers. The furniture was in the Louis Quatorze style; chairs had high carved backs. There were Chelsea figures, a sideboard full of plate, a Japan cabinet, a Kidderminster carpet, huge brass andirons. In such rooms the unbroken link between the Old World and the New was maintained.

As Squire Effingham would have been the first to admit, politics can have a profound effect not only on the mind but the stomach. After the French alliance of 1778 many colonists adopted the fashionable cuisine of America's European ally. French soups, salads, bonbons and fricassees were the order of the day. General Washington was served by a steward of French extraction; later on Jefferson brought a French cook to the White House. During Monroe's administration the food-minded minister De Neuville delighted to have Southern planters try his inventions; celery shaped like oysters, puddings in the forms of fowls, codfish disguised in a salad, for instance. So pervasive was this Francophilia that in the 1830's the German visitor Lieber observed that Americans had "engrafted French cookery upon the English." Some of the fancy dishes didn't hold up well, however, in the days before refrigeration. At one of the Washington's lordly plantation dinners, Mrs. Morris found that the cream had soured in the dessert. When she whispered the news to the General he immediately changed his plate. "But Mrs. Washington," the visitor noted in her diary, "ate a whole heap of it!" Patriots' souls were tried in many different ways. But judging from accounts of the lavish dinners given at Mount Vernon, the Washingtons usually ate very well indeed. At one such dinner, during Washington's presidency, one of the famous Italian dishes—spaghetti—was introduced to America.

The frontier housewife in James Fenimore Cooper's *Chainbearer* spoke for most families when she said: "I hold a family to be in a desperate way when the mother can see the bottom of the pork barrel. Give me the children that's raised on good sound pork afore all the game in the country. Game's good as a relish and so's bread; but pork is the staff of life."

All parts of the hog were relished. Spare ribs, backbones, ribs, and sausage were eulogized by Southerners. Plain people were content with chitterlings, cracklings, pig's feet, and jowls. Bacon was used to supply the flavor for string beans, black-eyed peas, turnip tops, poke, mustard, and collards. Juice left in the container after the vegetables were removed—called "pot likker"—was said to have magical nutritive values. A whole line of politicians, including Huey Long, have publicly extolled the unmatched virtues of corn pone and "pot likker."

No self-respecting pig can imagine a higher distinction than becoming, in due course, a Virginia ham—spicy as a woman's tongue, sweet as her kiss, tender as her love. The Virginia (or Tidewater) ham dates back to the mid-seventeenth century when English piglets got loose and began to savor the local products—especially peanuts. Called "earth chocolate," peanuts had been transplanted to Africa as a cheap food on slave ships; back in Virginia, they were excellent fodder for pigs turned out to root in the sandy fields. This gave hams a unique flavor which no one who has ever been exposed to can forget. Let those who prefer Tennessee country ham backed with pickled peaches, Texas ham with corn meal coating, Georgia country ham, glazed sugar-coated ham with champagne sauce, Gertrude Carraway's Carolina ham, fried Kentucky ham with red gravy, Alabama ham loaf with mustard sauce, or Florida ham with cayenne pepper argue their cases. All one has to do to be completely won over to Virginia is to *eat* it.

Anyone who has read this far (let alone slipped off to sample a thin slice of ham) must be thirsty by now. Consider, for a moment, American drinking habits. As has already been broadly hinted, drinking is both a favorite indoor and outdoor sport in the Four Kingdoms (tobacco, cotton, rice, and sugar). Hot weather, traditions, and natural inclination all point the way. No less a figure than the Father of our Country capitalized on this fact when he ran for office. During the 1758 elections in Frederick County, Washington's agent supplied 160 gallons to the 391 qualified voters and "unnumbered hangers-on." The supporters of Washington were asked to choose not only between candidates but spirits. Rum, punch, wine, beer, and cider royal flowed. Washington won handily.

Eschewing the smoother and lighter drinks of outlanders, Southerners have remained true to corn whiskey, sometimes given the more elegant name first used by Captain George Thorpe at Jamestown in 1622—bourbon. The distillers in Maryland and Kentucky are generally considered proper sources; although in periods of great stress (Prohibition, for example) mountain stills are considered adequate. Hardly a man in the back country fails to respond with a wink if you ask him where you can get a little corn likker, moonshine, white lightnin', or rot gut.

Distilled corn has seen Southerners through good days and bad. One of the colorful characters in the War between the States was Major Chatham Roberdeau Wheat, leader of the Louisiana Tigers. There he was, waiting to fight the enemy. In one hand he held a glass of bourbon, in the other his Mother's prayer book. He was partaking deeply of both.

The fame and flavor of bourbon have won many outside the region; but some mixed drinks are inextricably bound with the South. The most famous is the mint julep. At this high shrine it is time for us to do homage.

Historians say the julep (or *julap*) originated in Persia, where it was a minted non-alcoholic fruit drink. Medical people still use the word to refer to a sweet demulcent mixture—but Southerners reserve it for livelier and more potent occasions. For them it must be, as a *sine qua non,* alcoholic and delectable. There is no agreement among them on how a "proper" mint julep should be made. But amphibious amateurs who smacked their lips at concoctions served at the Mansion House in ante-bellum Natchez put up an impressive case. Having done considerable research on this whole matter, in books and bottles, I am casting my lot with this prescription:

> Take a large and deep cut glass tumbler, fill it
> with sufficient sugar and ice to the brim—half
> of the ice shaved into snow and the rest in lumps
> of moderate size. Lay on the top of it three

fresh leaves of mint without any part of the stem attached. Pour on just half a glass of fine unimpeachable cognac brandy, then just half a glass of fine old Jamaica rum; then add half a glass of old ripe port wine. Then pour the mass rapidly for some time, back and forth in two tumblers; the longer this action continues, the better. Then plant a small bunch of mint on one side of the tumbler by putting the stems down into the ice, and having the leaves up about as high as the nose of the drinker should come. Now—drink up!

Even as I put words to paper I can hear the contentious uproar. Kentuckians will be gathering and swearing that the insult just done to their bourbon whiskey calls for revenge. The julep must be prepared only in a *silver* goblet. The mint leaf must be crushed gently between the thumb and forefinger, the goblet nearly filled with shaved ice. Then add all the bourbon the goblet will hold. A few mint sprigs should decorate the top, after it has been frapped with a spoon. A straw is strictly forbidden. It must be sipped.

Sipping a julep isn't a bad way to end a chapter, or an evening, or a meal. Oh yes, we have produced our writers, philosophers, statesmen—but also the lowly goober, hamhock, and crushed mint. They will be popular long after you and I have left the scene.

18. HEGEL IN HOLLYWOOD

Opinion is like a pendulum, and obeys the same law.

—Arthur Schopenhauer

Topsy, you will remember, "jes' growed." This little black savage, known colloquially as a pickaninny (Webster called that "pidgin English" in the Bad Old Days) emerged from Uncle Tomsville where (except during ice storms) a good time was had by all.

But gone are the good-bad days. The term "Tom" is worse than any known four-letter word, and Topsy has become groovy. She comes on as one of the Supremes, with a dress the likes of which no professor's wife dares dream; she is all Black Baroque, and beautiful.

And Tom's descendant is nowhere to be found. He is locked in the bathroom, splashing in the bathtub, teaching a few of his willing female students (black and white) the glories of knowing Superstud.

From Shafted to Shafter in half a century: behold the history of black stereotypes on America's silver screen.

Is there anywhere, in popular culture, a better demonstration of Hegelian truth? Once the pendulum has swung far enough to one extreme, it returns not to a middle position, but the opposite extreme. To every thesis, an antithesis. Before World War II, according to the celluloid evidence, black men could do nothing right. Now, in the 1970's, they can do nothing wrong. How did this come to be? Might we deduce, from a close look at this specific and timely sector of our culture, some principle that might help us understand the culture as a whole? Is the history of black film stereotypes paralleled by that of other groups in society, or by films in other cultures? If, as the old cliche would have it, Hollywood is our dream factory, who and how can we interpret those dreams?

To analyze a set of stereotypes, on or off film, is no easy task. Art and life are not separated by any innate quality of value: only by particular standards we seek to impose. Art can never be encompassed by canons of personal taste or nomenclature, but only products of man the maker. What man can make or imagine is not restricted by his color. Hence we can only give a guarded answer to the seemingly simple question, "Where does American black popular culture begin?" An evasive, if at least defensible answer might be: at the place and time when black men began to live, breathe, and create on American soil. Much of it, by its very nature, was neither preservable nor preserved—mainly oral, not written; casual, not formal; clandestine, not overt. Africans brought to this country were a foreign people, whose customs, attitudes, and desires were shaped to a different place and a radically different life. Keeping this fact in mind, one sees many aspects of the black-white film encounter in a totally different way. Much that purports to be humorous is in fact tragic.

That so many blacks made their mark in films suggests that (in the arts, at least) there was not a complete antithesis. Art, being a universal language, overcomes even great ethnic and political barriers. This too had been shown long before the Movie Era, when Congo Square in New Orleans (later famed as the birthplace of jazz) rocked to the master drums of Africa. As late as the nineteenth century, pure African songs could be heard and pure African dances seen in the southern United States. African tradition was even more deeply rooted in Haiti, Guiana, Cuba, and Brazil. These places are also, in the larger meaning of the term, part of American black popular culture and of the lifestyle depicted on films.

As Seigfried Kracauer notes in *Theory of Film: The Redemption of Physical Reality* (1960), any nation's films are fully understandable only in relation to actual psychological patterns of that nation. Both movie makers and audiences engage in muted dialogues on the nature of social forms and formulae. Films are, among many other things, mechanisms of social integration, transmitters of popular ideas, confirmers of stereotypes. We believe in what appears on the screen because it confirms what we believe before we see it.

The great physical and historical reality, in the case of Black Americans, is chattel slavery. Not until the Civil War ended in 1865 did the 4,000,000 ex-slaves join the 400,000 free Negroes and 27 million non-Afro-Americans in enjoying the benefits of liberty. Much of the behavior of Americans (white and black, north and south, young and old) is understandable only against this background.

"Uncle Tom," comes right out of this history. Harriet Beecher Stowe's *Uncle Tom's Cabin* (1852) had an enormous vogue not only in America, but around the world. When she went abroad, the reception given to the American author of the famous attack on slavery was little short of hysterical. She had become a symbol.

Uncle Tom, the long-suffering, subservient slave, loved even those who hated and abused him. Ever since, "Tom" has symbolized one who chooses not to fight back; to remain faithful even to those who destroy him. The infant movie industry managed to produce a 12-minute "Uncle Tom's Cabin" as early as 1903. In it Tom (played by a famous black minstrel star, Sam Lucas) died in the arms of his white master. In the second motion picture version (1913), Tom was played by a white actor, Harry Pollard; a black actor, James Lowe, played the title role in the 1926 production—but in a way that would be acceptable to the white audience.

Artistic performance can never be divorced from political reality. During the years of the early films, Jim Crow laws were spreading throughout America and the temporary gains made during the Reconstruction period were being wiped out. Historians point out that 22 blacks from the South served with distinction between 1870 and 1901. The last of these, Representative George H. White of North Carolina, said, "We are forging ahead, slowly perhaps." But the analysis of Booker T. Washington, given in an 1895 Atlanta speech, might have been more accurate: "It is at the bottom of life we must begin, and not at the top."

Decades would pass before blacks would come to the top of the infant film industry. The fawning spineless Toms—sometimes called Billy, Sam, or Boy—would continue (on film, and frequently in real life) to accept second-class citizenship and back seats on buses. Implicitly they would accept the explanation white racists said stemmed from the Holy Bible itself: that Negroes were outcasts among the earth's people, descendants of Noah's son Ham, cursed by God and doomed to be servants forever.

The most persistent and pervasive black stereotype, on and off the screen, was Sambo. This living reversal of the American success story was lazy, stupid, unchanging; superstitious, childish, irresponsible. For centuries he has appeared in plays, novels, joke books, dime novels, animated cartoons, movies; on post cards, labels, radio shows, and television. An appendage of white attitudes, he was known for his shuffle and grin. Once he was a symbol, the image became its own reward, and continued without let-up. The essence of Sambo stressed by Clifton in Ralph Ellison's novel, *Invisible Man*:

Shake it up! Shake it up!
He's Sambo, the dancing doll, ladies and gentlemen
Shake him stretch him by the neck and set him down,
He'll do all the rest. Yes!

Two generations of movie-goers laughed at Black Sambo, in various shapes, sizes, and ages. He mispronounced words, pranced before stage lights, yassuhed his superiors, and grinned for the white folks. You could find him picking cotton on a postal card, smiling at you from a syrup bottle at breakfast time, poised in a horse-rider's costume on middle-class lawns in a mini-statue. "We like to picture the Negro as grinning at us," Bernard Wolfe has noted. "And his grin, as we see it—as we create it—always signifies a gift."

The man who put this filmic stereotype deep into the American psyche—as well as that of the Evil Mulatto and the Embattled Suthron —was David W. Griffith. White liberals have (for obvious and good reasons) made him the whipping boy of the Bad Old Days, all but rewriting Scott's lines to read:

> Breathes there a man with soul so dead
> Who never to himself has said
> D. W. makes my face turn red!

What made *Birth of a Nation* (1915) so bad was that it was so good—a masterpiece of cinematography, a real work of art. Politics and morality aside, one has only to see the "answer" to Griffith's film—the 1919 production called *Birth of a Race*—to verify this point. Never mind that Griffith continued to think of himself as a fair-minded person, whose *Intolerance* (1916) was a plea for brotherhood, using Walt Whitman's "cradle endlessly rocking" as its leitmotif. Griffith seems not so much to have invented as to have confirmed widespread white beliefs of his generation. It was his genius that has made him such a visible target.

A whole stream of post-Griffith mulattos has flowed through Hollywood: this tradition of the human being trapped in a racist No Man's Land, society's victim, caught between worlds but at home in neither, continued too. Famous examples were Nina Mae McKinney, especially for the Jeanne Eagels' role in *Rain*; and Fredi Washington in *Pinky* and *The Lower Depths*. *Pinky* centered on the "passing for white" theme, and also starred Ethel Waters and Frederick O'Neal, the first Negro to be elected president of Actors Equity. The mulatto role was also ably filled by Dorothy Dandridge (perhaps the most publicized black woman in the history of American movies, and the first to appear on the cover of *Life* magazine) and Lena Horne, who was once refused a room in a hotel that had booked her as a star.

The other major black female stereotype was Mammy—the tough, big-bosomed female who took no nonsense from anybody, and held both black and white families together with her grit and integrity. Steady and imperturbable, she provided the real backbone. Of one of the great literary portrayals in this mold, William Faulkner's Dilsey, Faulkner himself wrote: "They endured."

The best-known visual representation was the red-bandanaed Aunt Jemima, who still, in the 1970's, smiles at millions of Americans from the cover of their pancake mix boxes. On the screen the most successful Mammy was Hattie McDaniels, who was quoted as saying: "It is better to earn $7,000 a week playing a servant than $7 a week *being* one." For her portrayal of Mammy in *Gone With the Wind,* she won an Oscar for the best supporting actress of 1939.

Looking back over the early film and sex stereotypes, the patterns are inescapable. The most consistent feature was the attack on the black man—who was usually reduced from manhood to "boy." Their boyish delight in stealing chickens and eating watermelons was literally insatiable. They rolled dice and their eyes, and stayed true to their traits in all circumstances. Of the making of Sambos, there was no end.

From the perspective of hindsight one is apt to condemn the writers, producers, and even actors of such early racist films. Yet few of the people involved were deliberately mean or inhuman; they simply did what they were hired to do: make movies that white audiences would patronize and enjoy. Laissez-faire capitalism was as apparent in the entertainment industry as in many others as young America grew. Filmmakers gave the people what they wanted. The silver screen was really a mirror to those watching it. To blame Hollywood is like breaking the mirror because the viewer doesn't like the image seen in it.

The history of blacks and whites who early perceived these stereotypes, and fought in vain to overthrow them, has still to be written. In such an account a special place of honor will go to Paul Robeson, the handsome and articulate All-American football player who did a dozen pioneering films showing real black people and situations.[1] Films like *Emperor Jones, Borderline, Sanders of the River,* and *Proud Valley* pointed towards a black cinema that is only now beginning to emerge.

While Robeson was striving for a new understanding, America was enjoying what William Schechter has called "a new Uncle Tomism."[2] Amos 'n' Andy began a 40-year run on radio in 1925, played by whites-in-blackface Freeman Gosden and Charles Correll. Blacks as talented as Hattie McDaniel and Manada Randolph added their voices. But the great image-maker was Lincoln Theodore Monroe

Andrew Perry, alias Stepin Fetchit. He made $2 million in 5 years during the middle 30's, ending up with 12 cars and 16 Chinese servants. What America got from it was a completely believable, laughable New Sambo, who assured them that separate and unequal was, after all, the only solution.

World War II was a catalyst that changed almost everything in the United States, including race relations. That so many black people were willing to fight racism in Europe, at the same time they were victims of it at home, did not escape the eyes of black and white leaders. The former felt that they could demand more from the country, and many of the latter were determined that they should get it. The wartime President, Franklin D. Roosevelt, was instrumental in starting in 1944 the Independent Citizens' Committee of the Arts, Sciences, and Professions (I.C.C.A.S.P.), which took a strong stand against Jim Crow and all forms of discrimination. Lena Horne, Hazel Scott, Bette Davis, and Frank Sinatra were among its leaders.

That same year the International Film and Radio Guild (I.F.R. G.) was formed, with these three announced basic aims and purposes:

1. To create an awareness of misrepresentations of minorities among theatre, film, and radio audiences.
2. To influence producers, directors, writers, and performers towards creating truthful, realistic, and democratic presentations òf minorities.
3. To watch carefully portrayals and presentations of minorities, and to guard against distortion of characters.

But of course the distortions, or at least the unexamined platitudes, continued. The big difference was that black performers whose alternative had been "accept stereotype or starve" began to demand and get other alternatives. Consider the case of Butterfly McQueen, the petite black actress with the squeaky voice who won immediate acclaim for her "maid part" in *Gone With the Wind* (1939). Once the comic maid mantle was thrust upon her, she seemed destined to wear it forever. Her role in *The Women* and *Cabin in the Sky* proved the point. But while working on *Mildred Pierce,* the diminutive

McQueen issued a statement that she would no longer accept the sort of parts she had been forced to play. She was determined to establish the right of her people to a just representation on the silver screen.

In the last twenty years these 5 demands have been stated, re-stated, and implemented by many leaders, black and white:

1. America can never really lead the "free world" if she does not give real freedom (not only political, but economic and artistic) to all Americans at home.
2. There are not only moral but economic reasons to open up a true black cinema.
3. More Negro capital should be invested in cinema owner-ship and management.
4. The near-monopoly of a few major Hollywood studios should and must be ended.
5. Blacks must get a more meaningful role on all the media, and should train black critics to handle such assignments.

Robeson's films were the exceptions; stereotypes were still the rule. As a protest against stereotyping, the National Association for the Advancement of Colored People (N.A.A.C.P.) established a Holly-wood unit to work with filmmakers in 1945. There were many gradual changes, and some immediate ones. For example, Metro-Goldwyn-Mayer abandoned plans to screen *Uncle Tom's Cabin*, and Twentieth-Century Fox retitled a film which was planned as *Ten Little Niggers* to *Ten Little Indians*. Other Black leaders, like William Grant Still, argued that all-Negro films (like *Cabin in the Sky* and *Stormy Weather*) tended to "glorify segregation," and forced studios to abandon them. A generation later Blacks would argue *for* all-black films, and even "glorify segregation" as "black aesthetic."

American movies in the 1950's tended to break away from black stereotypes, and present roles with much greater sensitivity and individuality. A new cycle of Negro-prejudice pictures was started with Stanley Kramer's *Home of the Brave*. The central character, a Negro soldier (James Edwards), suffers a breakdown after a harrow-ing raid during World War II; but we later discover that his neurosis was caused by the racial prejudice of a comrade who called him "nigger." In quick succession such problem-films as *Lost Boundaries, Intruder in the Dust,* and *No Way Out* were receiving wide attention. In *Lost Boundaries,* a small New England town decides to accept a black doctor who has "passed" the color line, thus putting humanity above bigotry. *Intruder in the Dust,* based on a William Faulkner novel, tells the story of a proud, defiant black man who prefers lynching to crawling. In the end he is not lynched and the white lawyer who saves him says of black Lucas: "Lucas wasn't in trouble. We were in trouble."

No Way Out introduced America to a brilliant new black actor, Sidney Poitier. Born in the Bahamas in 1924, educated in Nassau, he came to New York at 16. After military service he studied theatre and made *No Way Out* in 1950. "Poitier is particularly good as the doctor who has to hurdle both his color and the exacting demands of his profession," critic Howard Barnes wrote in the *New York Herald Tribune.* Pursued by a psychopathic criminal-racist, Poitier has to show real strength to preserve his life. The black-white ghetto confrontation in the picture foreshadowed what would happen in several American cities in the 1960's. After outstanding performances in *Cry the Beloved Country, Blackboard Jungle,* and *Something of Value,* Poitier skyrocketed to fame in *The Defiant Ones* (1958). Centering on two prisoners chained together (one white, one black), the movie stresses the belief in decency and brotherhood. For this role Poitier was nominated for an Academy Award and the Berlin Film Festival Award. Subsequent performances in *Lilies in the Field, A Patch of Blue,* and *Guess Who's Coming to Dinner* added to his stature; surely here was a man acclaimed for his acting, not his race.

A new poignancy and artistry, on the much-presented theme of racism, was reached in Robert Mulligan's *To Kill a Mockingbird* (1962). By contrasting the deep prejudices of adults in a small town with the innocence of two children (those of the lawyer defending a black man accused of rape), the picture brought real drama where once there had been only cliche. Now the small town south began to appear as the villain—not the blacks persecuted there. In *The Chase* (1966), Lillian Hellman shows a Texas town full of bigotry, fanaticism, and prejudice. *In the Heat of the Night* (1967) shows an equally wretched Mississippi town, with a redneck police chief who became a kind of white cliche in this decade.

By now, however, the notion of brotherhood and reconciliation was being pushed aside in America. Both John F. Kennedy and Martin Luther King were assassinated, and black men everywhere decided that force must be met with force. Black Power became the new slogan. The cry of "Burn Baby Burn" was heard throughout the land. Once again the film which is the culture's mirror reflected these changes. These same films have also played an important role in the development of black consciousness.

"Non-violence is dead—it was killed in Memphis," a black militant says in *Up Tight*, produced by Jules Dassin in 1968. "You bled my Momma, you bled my Poppa—but you won't bleed me!" the black chorus screams in Melvin Van Peeples' *Sweet Sweetback's Baadasssss Song*. Directed by a shrewdly angry man, the film indicates that America had come full turn since *Birth of a Nation*. In the 1915 film, every black man had been hopelessly stereotyped; now, in 1971, the same could be said of every white man.

Van Peeples' protagonist, outlaw from the Los Angeles ghetto, brutally kills two policemen (known collectively as the Man) en route to Mexico. "The message of *Sweetback*," Van Peeples was quoted as saying in the August 16, 1971 issue of *Time,* "is that if you can get it together and stand up to the Man, you can win." What might be questioned here is the definition of winning.

By 1970 the idea of a black cinema was no mere pipe dream—it was a reality. Al Freeman, Jr., directed and starred in *A Fable* (1971), a bitter anti-white movie based on LeRoi Jones' play *Slave*. *The Bus is Coming* (1971), produced in the Watts area of Los Angeles tells the story of the militant Black Fists, who resolve to revenge the death of a nonviolent black killed by a white policeman. Once again the whites are the villains. The director, Wendell Franklin, was the first black admitted to the Screen Directors Guild.

Still another militant black film produced in 1971, *Black Chariot,* was underwritten by the black population of California. Not only the investment of 24 limited partners, but personal loans made to the producing firm through widespread soliciting of black communities, made the film possible.

International aspects of Negritude and black peoples were stressed by a number of films oriented towards Afro-American ties. The outstanding black American actor and playwright, Ossie Davis, went to Nigeria to direct *Kongi's Harvest* in 1971, for example. Americans played leading roles at the African Festival of the Arts in Dakar, Senegal in 1966, and at many other such meetings. More and more American automobiles carried "Afro" bumper stickers, with the red, green, and black colors of Black Liberation.

All this had wide economic as well as political implications. By 1970, it was estimated that Blacks comprised nearly one-third of American movie-goers; and the purchasing power of the black population stood near $40 billion annually. In areas where white products couldn't succeed, black ones might; for example, *Look* and *Life* failed, but the black equivalent, *Ebony*, continued to flourish. This was a significant cultural phenomena of the 1970's.

So was the rise of a highly successful New Black Cinema, heralded when the experimental *Cotton Comes to Harlem* was released in 1970. Directed by Ossie Davis and co-starring Godfrey Cambridge and Raymond St. Jacques, the film grossed more than $9 million; within two years 50 "black" movies had flooded the market, often imitative of earlier "white" successes. Among them was a black *Dracula* (*Blacula*), the radical slave saga (*Legend of Nigger Charlie*), a black western (*Buck and the Preacher*), a black dee jay story (*Melinda*), black boxer (*Hammer*), and a black thriller (*Slaughter*). A new vogue was also ushered in—the "Black Superstud" craze.

The outstanding example was *Shaft* (1971), which starred Richard Roundtree as an invincible hard-hitting private detective who could laugh, love, fight, and prevail better than any man, black or white. He reminded some of the white superstud, James Bond—007 raised to a new (black) power.

Soon *Shaft* suits, watches, belts, sunglasses, decals, and after shaving lotion flooded the market. Director Gordon Parks, Jr. summed it up: "Studios make films to get people to see them on whatever basis they're on. And if someone is going to put their money in a project, they expect a return." In this case, they got it. *Shaft* grossed $15 million.

Equally successful was the 1972 film *Super Fly*—a slang term for the "best dope" or drugs around. The hero, portrayed by Ron O'Neal, is a cocaine seller named "Priest," who decides to leave the racket after a super-deal which will bring him $1 million. Aided by two mistresses (one white, one black), hired killers, and generous applications of drugs, he overcomes all opposition and gets his million.

Not all black leaders applauded. Junius Griffin called it "an insidious film which portrays the black community at its worst, glorifying dope-pushers, pimps, and grand theft." The Rev. Jesse Jackson, head of Operation PUSH, ordered a boycott of the film which glamorized a black man who exploits his own people and gets away unharmed. In moving from Stepin Fetchit to "Super Nigger," *Ebony* commented in the December, 1972 issue, black film portraits had come full circle. Moses Gunn, who co-starred in both *Shaft* and its sequel, *Shaft's Big Score,* was quoted in that issue as saying: "I'm determined not to do another. I did the first two pictures because I thought my character (Bumpy) was real enough to portray; but one real cat in a movie full of caricatures isn't worth a damn."

What does this sudden upsurge in black film-making mean? Is it (in *Ebony*'s phrase) a "giant con game," or are we witnessing the birth of another creative chapter in film history? Are the blacks once again victims of a white establishment bent on thought-control? Is *Super Fly* in the final analysis more admirable than Uncle Tom? History suggests that "cultural explosions" can leave ditches as well as mountains. But we are too close to present-day affairs to make historical judgments.

The "magnolia myth" of smiling, contented darkies was well-rooted in American soil; it withered slowly, and even yet has not entirely died. But other myths have grown and flourished.

Can we balance the record without adding new and eventually equally questionable distortions? The problem of Hegel's pendulum, moving from one extreme to the other, applies to film history as well as to economics. But if the pendulum swings wildly in the 1970's, so it will be. "There is a tendency born of neglect to over-emphasize the importance of the Negro in America," historian Alan Conway writes with perspective gained from living in New Zealand. "If this is a fault then it is a fault on the right side to compensate for years of neglect and underrating."[3]

If a single man emerges as something of a villain in this rapid leap through many years and hundreds of movies, it is David W. Griffith, who conceived and directed *Birth of a Nation.* Yet this is the same man who said, in 1917:

> The cinema camera is the agent of Democracy.
> It levels barriers between races and classes.

The use of that camera, and the other devices at our command, will continue to be one of the most sensitive and meaningful aspects of American civilization. What we see on the screen is ourselves—writ large. No man of good will can be happy with all that has been seen there since Topsy "jes' growed." The metamorphosis of the film industry, like that of Topsy herself, is a marvel to behold. It indicates how much more complex a subject popular culture is than either supporters or critics have yet realized. We are just setting out, like some latter-day Darwin, on our long journey to collect data. Whether we can devise new laws of evolution and forms of classification, remains to be seen.[4]

19. NORTH STAR

Since we mount high arts on the popular ones, one can
see how basic this ground is for any scholar.

—Marshall McLuhan

There he stands: courtly, tweedy, intense. You are on Canada's
Do Line, facing the North Star. This is Marshall McLuhan.

"Let's go to my office," he says. Just what will it be like—the
place where those books which altered your life, and so many others,
originated; where one day he jotted on a piece of paper, "The medium is the message"? Or on another, "The earth is a burnt-out missile
cone"?

We walk around and behind the splendid sturdy buildings that
make up the University of Toronto. The Centre for Culture and
Technology is housed in a shabby old coach house, in a muddy flat
behind a newer building. We reach it by walking over a narrow
wooden catwalk, through which mud oozes after a recent rain.

"Be careful," the Media Messiah says, "Don't skid." He smiles
and does what he enjoys the most—puns. "Skid's Row."

I cannot help recalling Tom Wolfe's much-quoted line on
McLuhan—the man doing a ballet on the catwalk: "Suppose he is
what he sounds like—the most important thinker since Newton?"

McLuhan is warmly greeted by staff members and secretaries,
as am I. His cluttered office has a green wall-to-wall carpet and an
orange sign which reads:

INFORM ALL THE TROOPS
THAT COMMUNICATION HAS
COMPLETELY BROKEN DOWN!

There is a large Marx Brothers poster and a rowing paddle labeled "Trinity Hall Rugger Boat–1936." The name "H. M. McLuhan" is in the third position on the list of names. Suspended from the ceiling by a string is this Latin inscription:

CAUSAE AD INVICEM CASSAE SUNT

That very British paddle and Latin inscription are keys to the man who talks so wisely and rapidly. He is the product of classical learning and elite Oxbridge education in the years before World War II; an English gentlemen working diligently in one of His Majesty's Dominions; never forgetting the creeds, codes, and concepts which became, long before many of his young admirers were born, part of his very being.

Later on we go to his home, a spacious 19th century structure in Toronto's suburb called Wychwood Park. His wife, a charming Texas lady, oversees the house and tries to see that her famous husband has some privacy and sufficient rest–no easy task. For another word which fits McLuhan is *puritanical.* He never stops working. "Work for me simply means keeping it on the back burner," he says. "I just wait for the right opportunity to pop, and to push the probe a bit further." The pushing is never-ending.

Neither is the courtliness. Like Sir Kenneth Clark, whom he resembles in many significant ways, he believes in manners, ritual, tradition and is, at the same time, one of the most "revolutionary" and controversial figures in communications and cultural studies.

If his personal conduct is set and predictable, McLuhan's attitude isn't. "I am an investigator," he says time and again. "I make probes. I have no point of view. I don't stay in one position. I talk back to media and set off an adventure of exploration."

Born in rural Canada in 1911, the tall thin lad studied engineering at the University of Manitoba before realizing a deep desire to attend Cambridge University in England. There he was converted to Catholicism—another key point in his philosophy. "It gives me emotional stability," he says. Would any of his class mates pulling an oar in that 1936 rugger boat have guessed he would be known later as Pop Daddy, High Priest of Popthink, Oracle of Electronics, the Metaphysical Wizard, A Belated Whitman Singing the Body Electric with Thomas Edison as Accompanist?[1]

By his own admission, McLuhan started out as an elitist. "Before I wrote the *Mechanical Bride*," he reports, "I had a moralistic approach to all environmental facts. I abominated machinery, cities, everything except the most Rousseauistic. Gradually I became aware of how useless this was and I discovered a different approach and I adopted it."[2] The good doctor began by healing himself.

Or did he, as Benjamin DeMott and Christopher Ricks say, simply give up any concern with distinguishing good from bad? That concern was central in *The Mechanical Bride,* but defiantly absent in *Understanding Media.* In the 1950's advertising appalled McLuhan; by 1964 he announced that "the ads are by far the best part of any magazine or newspaper." Such reversals prompt DeMott to call him "the pardoner of his age—a purveyor of perfect absolution for every genuine kind of modern guilt," offering "ultimately, the release from consciousness itself."

If one extends such criticism beyond McLuhan to Pop Culture, he has leveled the most disturbing long-range challenge which we must meet.

A contemporary of McLuhan who comes in for the same type of professional criticism is Arnold Toynbee. Both work in patterns so much larger and free-wheeling than most of their colleagues that they elicit but seldom get a different type of appraisal.[3] In the world of finely-honed scalpels they use the broadsword. A lot of blood is spilled.

Beginning with the phonetic alphabet and the Greeks, McLuhan argues, there emerged in Western civilization a mode of detachment and noninvolvement. From this refusal to be involved in the world he lived in, literate man became alienated from his environment, even from his body. He valued the isolated, delimited self, particularly the mind. Today we have entered a relatively dim, unconscious world in which the electronic extensions of everyone's nerves involves him deeply in all other lives. While writing and print technology tore man out of the group-creating the great misery of psychic alienation-suddenly and without warning the electronic media hasten him back into the embrace of the group.

Electronic media have created a global village in which all information can be shared, simultaneously, by everyone; where all walls between peoples, art, thoughts, come tumbling down. In this environment the problem becomes one of data selection and procession.

Formerly, work was in direct relation to the source of available energy. Man scratched only the earth's surface for resources. Electric energy allows us to create our own environments, as artists create theirs. Suddenly everybody and everything is involved in transforming the environment into a work of art. The world is a throbbing assemblage of *things* that communicate. The Black Age (coal, mines, factories, soot) is going. The White Age (electricity, air travel, glass houses, computers) is here. With the sense of sight, the idea communicates the emotion.

The Electronic Age is returning oral and tribal culture to the West. We are being hurled back into the tribal and oral pattern with its seamless web of kinship and interdependence. Speech over writing, the primitive over the civilized: is McLuhan trotting out that old 18th century hero, the Noble Savage? Yes—but in a new model, with electronic devices which make writing and speech unnecessary for communication. McLuhan does not defer to great men or exemplars of the past. For him the real heroes of the human drama are not men but media.

Hence his chapters do not center on Washington, Lincoln, or Kennedy, but Money ("The Poor Man's Credit Card"), Photographs ("Brothels without Walls"), and Movies ("The Reel World"). For him media do extraordinary things, altering the total social temperature. "Since TV," he writes, "the whole American political temperature has cooled down, down, down, until the political process is almost approaching *rigor mortis.*" This, and not the politicians, is what interests him most about American politics.

Nor are the inventors or perfectors of media special idols. Alexander Graham Bell had no idea how the telephone would change modern life—his personal story does not interest McLuhan. The drama of history is a pageant whose inner meaning is man's metamorphosis through media. The medium is the message, the focus. When men *do* achieve fame, they ride on technological tides like driftwood thrown up onto the beach. "Any phrasemaking yokel can become a world center."

For McLuhan "cool," refers not to people but media. To be "cool" is to be poorly defined and low on data—cartoons, telephone, television. To be "hot," on the other hand, is to be highly-defined and full of data—photographs, radio, movie. The TV image is of low intensity and does not afford (as does the film) detailed information about objects. The viewer is forced to participate.

Hot and *cool* are not classifications but structural forms—terms from the musical world where they have high, structural meaning. The hotting up of one sense leads to hypnosis; the cooling off of all senses to hallucination. One can extend his hot-cool dichotomy over into the real world of people:

HOT	COOL
Phonetic alphabet	Ideogram
City	Hillbilly
Waltz	Bugaloo
Hitler	Stalin
"Hard sell"	"Soft sell"

Is it an accident, he asks, that the narcissistic heroes like Tarzan, Superman, Cowboys, and Sleuths are weak on social life? Intrigued by the tart, anti-heroic pose of film-star Humphrey Bogart, reminiscent of the 19th century poetry of A. E. Houseman, he asks (with his own brand of "cool"), "Is Bogart America's Shropshire Lad?"

He *has* explored quite thoroughly, James Joyce, T. S. Eliot, Ezra Pound, and Thomas Nashe. Like them, he is fascinated with words, innuendoes, and puns. To pun is to consolidate by pounding or ramming down (as earth or rubble, in making a roadway). He has never sought popular support or acclaim; like Eliot, he thinks writers require not a large but a significant audience. When the *Gutenberg Galaxy* appeared McLuhan got both. What the French call *le McLuhanisme* went into orbit. It is still circling the globe; its *beep beep beep* is the new shot heard round the world. Brightly shines the North Star.

20. FINAL STROLL

In the end is my beginning.

—T. S. Eliot

Nowhere does one feel the power, speed, and ruthlessness of our culture more than on a superhighway; no icon of that culture is more valid than the automobile. I decide to put my final thoughts together while walking along the grassy shoulders of I-95.

Immediately I feel helpless and afraid. Small cars loom up as monsters, hurling forward, hissing and snarling. Any one of them, by swerving slightly, could snuff out my life. Even more terrifying are the drivers' faces, etched with anger and antagonism. Take a ride or walk "for pleasure"? Not in this environment. The scene is rigged for instant tragedy.

Popular culture is like Henry Adams' famous electrified wire: we cannot survive by holding to it, yet we cannot turn it loose. No matter what we think about I-95, we will depend on and speed on it —tomorrow and tomorrow and tomorrow. . . .

Our cars won't lose their power—but our myths have. What was once sacred now seems silly. A dread disease is upon us: we are being demythologized. To survive is to remythologize. I am walking along this highway today not so much to discover a new mythos as to participate in it.

Striding forward, I feel outmoded;—anachronistic;—slightly ridiculous. What are *you*, a full-grown, sensible, successful American,

162

doing *walking* along the highway? What will people think (especially
any who happen to know you)? That there is an emergency—your
car was stopped, you abandoned it. Suppose somebody, drunk on
the milk of human kindness, trys to stop? "Eighteen-Car Pile-Up on
Turnpike," the headline will read. "Ambulances Unable to get to
Victims in Freak Accident." Maybe one ought to wear sun-glasses,
so no one will recognize him; or take his tie off, so no one can possibly spot an ambulating Establishment professor slightly off his
rocker.

Shades, no tie, highway-walking: what will the next state cop
think when he spots you? The world's oldest Hippie? A dispossessed
pusher who's been pushed out of somebody's car? An escaped
prisoner who abandoned or wrecked a stolen car?

Of course he'll stop, walk over with that pistol bouncing on his
hip, look at you with those steel-gray eyes, and say, "O.K., feller, get
in the front seat. Don't cause any trouble. I want to talk to you."
What will he say when I explain why I'm strolling along I-95?

Two trucks roar by, carrying six cars like baby kangaroos in the
pouch. How many horsepower, altogether, on those two vehicles?
More horses than the U. S. Cavalry used to rout a good-sized Indian
tribe in the 1850's. What will these sleek steel monsters be used for?
In a month six dainty dieting housewives, weighing in at 98 pounds
each, will be driving them from Suburbia to Supermarket to pick up
a carton of Diet Colas—325 horses working for half an hour to corner
two quarts of colored water.

Nervously you take your eyes off the juggernauts (breathing
no fire from their mouths but plenty of pollution from their tail pipes)
and glance at the gully to the right. Drivers go too fast to see what
you see: the charnel house of civilization.

Bent hub caps, squashed cans, paper bags, pop bottles, orange
skins, stretched prophylactics, blown-out rubber tires, decapitated
doll-babies—the butt ends of a million smokes and a thousand dreams.
T. S. Eliot found the phrase for Europe between World Wars: *The
Waste Land.* John Kouwenhoven's book title epitomizes America
since World War II: *The Beer Can Alongside the Highway.*

To hell with the beer cans—what about the people? Alongside

the highway they are traffic problems. Inside the cars they become bits of protoplasm guiding tons of metal through space. On the assembly line they are humanized ants, methodically producing too many cars for too few roads—which become instantly obsolescent.

I think of a newspaper story about Little Eddie. The investigating doctor reported that Eddie carried with him an elaborate life-support system made up of tubes, bulbs, and wheels. At meals he ran imaginary wires from a wall socket to himself so his food could be digested. His bed, like his Dad's car, was rigged up with batteries, head lights, and direction signals.

Autistic fantasy? Or Everyman growing up so he can make it on I-95? Little Eddie and the Big Bribe: everyone can claim every scientific advance and every material advantage, as long as everyone takes everything offered in the quantity that the system requires.

On this formula the whole pop panorama becomes a single environment, a single mosaic: billboards, supermarkets, communes, concubines, comics, hot dogs, cold turkey, Watergate, Da Nang, Shangri La. Not only related, but sequential and predictable. Cornucopia Unlimited.

Abundance: the Sorcerer's Apprentice of post-Hiroshima America. Nobody loves a fat man. In the mythology of Western man, good guys have big biceps, bad guys big stomachs. Caesar's muscles ripple as he invades Gaul. Sweat pours off Nero's second chin as Rome burns. Later on Caesar was so abundantly successful that Cassius asked:

> Upon what meat doth this our Caesar eat
> That he hath grown so fat?

Even lovable buffoons like Falstaff (who lards the lean earth) are rejected by reformed Prince Hal. How can one who fails to control his own appetite control anything else?

Scarcity smacks not only of the heroic, but the holy. The three religions that have most shaped modern civilization (Christianity, Judaism, and Islam) came out of the desert—from fasting, famine, and poverty. Holy men scorn earthly pleasures, mortify their bodies,

denounce opulent neighbors. John the Baptist's wardrobe consisted
largely of animal skins, his diet of grasshoppers. Jesus said the poor
are always with us, and went to the desert to fast and pray. Self-
denial remains the most impressive gesture a leader can make.
India's independence came not when Mahatma Ghandi insisted on
fighting, but when he refused to eat.

Over the centuries the idea that wickedness is the handmaiden
of abundance has been widely accepted. Since there never has been
enough to go around, anyone with extra portions must either have
inherited it (he is undeserving) or appropriated it (he is unloving).
The history of democratic thought is the unending struggle to overthrow kings, robber barons, and tyrants—to see that government is
run for the many, not the few. But what happens when (to quote
Emerson), "Things are in the saddle/And ride mankind?" What
happens when abundance becomes a mindset—a national consciousness, bolstered by government, business, education, and mythology?

Charles Reich attempts to answer in *The Greening of America*,
one of the hopeful spring blooms in 1971. "We may be in the grip
not of capitalist exploiters," he writes, "but of mindless, impersonal
forces that pursue their own, non-human logic." *Zoom*—those forces
speed past me, heavier, bigger, more threatening than the little
people who attempt to steer them. Never mind, Reich counsels, the
machine will self-destruct. The chromobile, fabulously expensive and
instantly obsolescent, will not prevail.

Reich, my stroll suggests, is wrong. The revolution I am observ-
ing is more basic than the one Reich posits. Consciousness I and II
may well give way to III, and then IV—but the wheels will not stop
rolling. People will *drive* to Woodstock. Many other "revolutions"
of our times—happenings and minimal in art, black or red liberation.
Amerika and counter-culture, may or may not outlast their highly
vocal founders. But these wheels. . . .

I don't deny the impact and sincerity of such movements. What
the young feel, and the media exploit, is real enough. What about
staying power? How does a fad become a trend, then a movement?

For surely the car—a fad in Ford's day, a trend in Wilson's, has
become a necessity, even a mania. In fact, a Long Island judge recently

gave "automania" a legal definition: an over-obsession with the automobile as a status symbol, as a means of getting some place in a hurry, as a vehicle for a flight from tensions, or to indulge in a craving to show off. The car has religious overtones, with doctrines and rituals all its own. There are wheels within wheels, cults within cults, *mystiques*, fetishes, gambits. Classic cars, foreign cars, sports cars, doodle bugs, hot rods . . . the holy rolling empire. With and in these cars we perform the rites of passage: separation, initiation, return. The car has refashioned all the spaces that unite and separate men.

But nothing can reshape the questions that unite and separate us—bring us together in life, and pull us apart in death. Might not these questions define the real parameters of popular culture?

As death approached, the popular legend holds, Gertrude Stein asked a number of her famous friends to gather at her bedside. "Does anyone have the answers?" she asked. Silence. "Very well, then," she said as the end approached, "why doesn't somebody ask the questions?"

★　　★　　★　　★

NOTES

PROLOGUE

[1] Benjamin DeMott, "The Culture Wars," in *Saturday Review,* May 20, 1972. For a fuller statement, see his book *Supergrow: Essays and Reports on Imagination in America* (New York, 1970).

[2] Robert Walker, *American Studies in the United States* (Baton Rouge, 1958), p. 8.

[3] Tremaine McDowell, *American Studies* (Minneapolis, 1948), p. 51.

[4] See, for example, Marshall Fishwick, *American Studies in Transition* (Philadelphia, 1964) and Ray Browne, Donald Winkelman, and Allen Hayman, *New Voices in American Studies* (Purdue University *Studies*, 1966).

[5] Robert Meredith, *American Studies: Essays on Theory and Method,* (Columbus, 1968), xii.

1. PARAMETERS

[1] Arthur A. Berger, *Li'l Abner: A Study in American Satire* (New York, Twayne, 1970), p. 28.

[2] I. A. Richards, *Principles of Literary Criticism* (London, Macmillan, 1924), p. 203.

[3] See Giuseppe Marchiori, *Arte e Artisti d'Avavguardia in Italia, 1910-1950* (Milano, 1960).

[4] Both essays are in the Winter 1967 issue of *Journal of Popular Culture,* which is published at Bowling Green University. The Friedenberg quote above is from p. 319 of the same issue. Continuing to open new areas for academic analysis, the *Journal* published "a stupendous death-defying extravaganza" in the Winter 1972 issue, featuring "Circuses, Carnivals, and Fairs."

2. WHALES

[1] Matthew Arnold, *Culture and Anarchy* (New York, 1966), p. 72.

[2] Bernard Mayo, *Jefferson Himself* (Boston, 1942), pp. 300-301.

[3] John Kouwenhoven, *Made in America* (New York, 1948), p. 125.

[4] "Beatles, Batman, and the New Aesthetic," *Midway*, Autumn, 1966, p. 68.

[5] *New York Times*, October 11, 1970, p. 88.

[6] My thinking here, and in other places, has been influenced by George Kubler's masterpiece, *The Shape of Time* (New Haven, 1960).

3. ROOTS

[1] Robert E. Rigel, "American Frontier Theory," *Cahiers d'Histoire Mondiale*, III, no. 2, 1956; p. 367.

[2] From the huge library of Turneriana, George Rogers Taylor's collection of essays on *The Turner Thesis Concerning the Role of the Frontier in American History* (Boston, 1949), is a good beginning point. Walter P. Webb's *The Great Frontier* (Boston, 1952) tries to put the idea into world perspective. In *Frontier: American Literature and the American West* (Princeton, 1965), Edwin Fussell attempts to show how the frontier "passed into American culture and became a formal principle in our literature."

[3] How did this interaction also form the media, stereotypes, and ethnicity on which popular culture is based? Little has been done to answer such a question; there are important clues in such books as C. R. Fish, *The Rise of the Common Man* (New York, 1927), Russel Nye, *The Unembarrassed Muse* (New York, 1970), and John Cawelti, *The Six-Gun Mystique* (Bowling Green, 1970).

[4] My thoughts are summarized in "The Cowboy: America's Contribution to the World's Mythology," *Western Folklore*, XI, April 1952; pp. 77 f. A recent comprehensive study is John Cawelti, *op. cit.*

[5] John Cawelti, *op. cit.*, p. 85.

4. HEROES

[1] Yonosuke Nagai, "The United States is Disintegrating," from *Psychology Today*, May, 1972; p. 26.

5. POP PRINCE

[1] Harold Faber, editor, *The Kennedy Years* (New York, 1964), p. 17.

[2] *Ibid.*, p. 136.

[3] Goddard Lieberson, editor, *John Fitzgerald Kennedy: As We Remember Him* (New York, 1965).

[4] Richard Rovere, "The Candidates," *New Yorker*, July 23, 1960.

[5] Gerald W. Johnson, "Once Touched by Romance," *The New Republic*, December 7, 1963.

6. CELEBRITIES

[1] So argues J. P. Priestly, "Marilyn Monroe," *Saturday Evening Post*, April 27, 1963; p. 12.

[2] See Penelope Houston, *The Contemporary Cinema* (London, 1968) and Andre Bazin, *What Is Cinema?* (Paris, 1968).

[3] Walter M. Gerson and Sander H. Lunc, "*Playboy* Magazine: Sophisticated Smut or Social Revolution," *Journal of Popular Culture*, 1:3, Winter, 1967; p. 220.

[4] This new involvement of man with man is the central concern of Walter Ong in *The Barbarian Within* (New York, 1964).

[5] For a detailed analysis see Patrick D. Hazard, "The Entertainer as Hero," *Journalism Quarterly* (Minneapolis, Minnesota), Spring, 1962.

7. ICONS

[1] See, for example, Leonid Ouspensky and Vladimir Lossky, *The Meaning of Icons* (Basel, Otto Walter, 1952).

[2] Robert Jay Lifton, "Protean Man," *Partisan Review,* Winter, 1968; p. 47.

[3] Harvey Cox's study of *The Secular City* (New York, 1965) argues that Biblical faith desacralizes the cosmos. The sacred always goes bad unless it is working with the secular. For more on this theme, and the switch to pop, see Gibson Winter, *The New Creation as Metropolis* (New York, 1963), Larry Shiner, *The Secularization of History* (New York, 1966), Kenneth Hamilton, *What's New in Religion?* (Grand Rapids, Michigan, 1968), and Marshall McLuhan, *Understanding Media* (New York, 1964)—especially chapter 32, "Weapons: War of the Icons."

[4] Claude Levi-Strauss, *The Savage Mind* (Chicago, University of Chicago Press, 1969), p. 47.

[5] See Jerome Bruner, *Essays for the Left Hand* (Cambridge, Harvard University Press, 1963) and Elli Maranda, *Myth and Art as Teaching Materials* (Cambridge, Educational Services, Occasional Paper No. 5, 1965).

[6] For a fuller discussion see Louis Kampf, *On Modernism: The Prospects for Literature and Freedom* (Cambridge, M.I.T. Press, 1968).

[7] This notion was set forth by Beaumont Newhall, a leading historian of photography, in a letter to the author dated April 21, 1969.

[8] See Mario Amaya, *Pop as Art* (London, Studio Vista, 1965) and Lucy R. Lippard, *Pop Art* (New York, Praeger, 1966).

[9] Susan Sontag uses these phrases in *Styles of Radical Will* (New York, Farrar, Straus, and Giroux, 1969).

9. BACK COUNTRY

[1] See Alexander H. Krappe, *The Science of Folklore* (London, Methuen, 1930), p. 70 f.

²The standard biography is Julia Collier Harris, *The Life and Letters of Joel Chandler Harris* (New York, 1918). This may be supplemented by consulting the sketch and bibliography in the Spiller-Thorp *Literary History of the United States* (New York, 1948).

³Quoted by Jay Hubbell in *The South in American Literature* (Dirham, 1954), p. 789.

⁴See for example, John Stafford's "Patterns of Meaning in Nights with Uncle Remus," *American Literature*, XVIII, May, 1946; T. H. English's "The Twice-Told Tale and Uncle Remus," *Georgia Review*, II, Winter 1948; and Louise Dauner's "Myth and Humor in the Uncle Remus Tales," *American Literature*, XX, May, 1948.

⁵Henri Peyre, "The Influence of Eighteenth Century Ideas on the French Revolution," *Journal of the History of Ideas*, X, 1949; p. 345.

⁶Richard Dorson, in *Journal of American Folklore*, 72, September, 1959; p. 202.

10. FAKELORE

¹See James Taylor Dunn, *The True, Moral, and Diverting Tale of the Cardiff Giant* (New York, 1948); A. C. Drummond and R. E. Card, *The Cardiff Giant* (Ithaca, Cornell University Press, 1949); and Louis J. Wolner, "David Hannum and the Cardiff Giant," *Cortland County Chronicles*, II, (Cortland, N. Y., 1958).

²See "A Theory for American Folklore; A Symposium," in *Journal of American Folklore*, 72, no. 285, September, 1959; p. 230.

³See Lewis Mumford, *The Golden Days* (New York, 1957), p. 29.

⁴For a specific and convincing verification of this point, see Herbert Passin and John W. Bennett, "Changing Agricultural Magic in Southern Illinois: A Systematic Analysis of Folk-Urban Transition," in *Social Forces*, 22, 1943; pp. 98-106.

⁵Letter to the author dated April 24, 1953. See Mr. Hyman's article in the *New York Folklore Quarterly*, June, 1953.

⁶George Grotz, *Instant Furniture Refinishing and Other Crafty*

Practices (New York, 1966), p. 21.

11. MOSAICS

[1] Guiseppe Bovini, *Ravenna Mosaics* (Greenwich, N.Y. Graphic Society, 1956), p. 6.

12. THEOLOGY

[1] For a full analysis, see these two books by Kenneth Hamilton: *God is Dead: The Anatomy of a Slogan* (1965) and *What's New in Religion? A Critical Study of New Theology, New Morality, and Secular Christianity* (1968). The files of *Christian Century* are also important.

[2] See Gibson Winter, *The New Creation as Metropolis* (1963) and Harvey Cox, *The Secular City* (1965) and *Feast of Fools* (1969).

13. MYTHOLOGY

[1] Marshall McLuhan and Barrington Nevitt, *Take Today: The Executive As Dropout* (Don Mills, Ontario, Longman Canada, 1972), p. 6.

[2] See "A Theory for American Folklore; A Symposium," in *Journal of American Folklore*, 72, no. 285, September, 1959; p. 230.

[3] See, for example, Keith Melville, *Communes in the Counter Culture: Origins, Theories, Styles of Life* (New York, Morrow, 1972); William Hedgepeth and Dennis Stock, *The Alternative: Communal Life in New America* (New York, Collier, 1970); and Richard Fairfield, *Communes USA: A Personal Tour* (Baltimore, Penguin, 1972).

14. GLOBES

[1] See Guiseppi Marchiori, *Arte e Artisti d'Avanguardia in Italia, 1910-1950* (Milano, 1960).
[2] See Irving and Harriet Deer, *The Popular Arts: A Critical Reader* (New York, 1967), pp. 4-9.
[3] Bernard Weinbaub, "Youths Flock to Kabul," in New York *Times*, May 30, 1973; p. 10.

15. TWO WALTS

[1] Peter and Linda Murray, *A Dictionary of Art and Artists* (London, 1965), p. 310.
[2] This argument is developed by Bates Lowry in *The Visual Experience* (New York, 1964).
[3] For a fuller account see chapter 15, "The Mouse is the Message," in my book on *The Hero: American Style* (New York, McKay, 1969).
[4] The only full scale study—and a largely unsympathetic one— is Richard Schickel, *The Disney Version: the Life, Times, Art and Commerce of Walt Disney* (New York, Scribner's, 1968). Christopher Finch's 1973 volume called *The Art of Walt Disney* is less probing.
[5] See Stith Thompson's *Motif-Index of Folk Literature* (Bloomington, Indiana, 1932-36), especially vol. Vi.; pp. 377 f.
[6] *National Geographic*, August, 1963; p. 207.

16. TWO WARS

[1] Frank E. Vandiver, "The Civil War: Its Theory and Practice," *The Texas Quarterly*, II, no. 2, Summer, 1959; p. 102.
[2] My diagnosis of "Civil War II" appeared in *The Texas Quarterly*, II, no. 2, Summer, 1959.
[3] See the New York *Times* for May 16, 1971.

18. HEGEL IN HOLLYWOOD

[1] See Thomas Cripps, "Paul Robeson and Black Identity in American Movies," in *Massachusetts Review,* Summer, 1970.

[2] William Schechter, *The History of Negro Humor in America* (New York, Fleet Press, 1969), ch. V.

[3] Alan Conway, *The History of the Negro in the U.S.A.* (London, 1968), p. 34.

[4] One encouraging sign is the appearance of articles and books on this subject by Black writers Gene Siskel's summary called "Caricature of Character: The Black Actor Evolves" appeared in the May 6, 1973 Magazine Section of the Chicago *Tribune,* and Donald Bogle's book called *Toms, Coons, Mulattoes, Mammies, and Bucks* was published by Viking Press that same month.

19. NORTH STAR

[1] To match these and other epithets with their coiners, see Gerald Stearn, ed., *McLuhan Hot and Cold: A Critical Symposium* (New York, 1967); and Raymond Rosenthal, *McLuhan: Pro and Con* (New York, 1968).

[2] *Op. cit.,* p. 295. The most important single source for McLuhan's "different approach" seems to have been Harold Innis' *The Bias of Communication,* which was published in 1951.

[3] One of the few scholars who shares McLuhan's basic typology and still works within a single area of thought (theology) is Walter J. Ong, S. J. His 1968 book *The Presence of the Word* insists that historical explanations according to media development can be reconciled with Christian historiography.

Recently Professor McLuhan has completed a revision of *Understanding Media,* in which the laws of the media are "stated axiomatically and structurally," and 40 new chapters are added.

THE AUTHOR

Marshall Fishwick has written about his native Virginia
(*Virginia: A New Look at the Old Dominion, Gentlemen of Virginia,
Lee After the War*); heroes (*American Hero: Myth and Reality, The
Hero, American Style, Heroes of Popular Culture*); heroines (*Jane
Addams, Clara Barton*); and the devil (*Faust Revisited*).

He has held Fulbright lectureships in Denmark, Germany,
Poland, and India, and has served as an American Specialist for the
Department of State. As Director of the Wemyss Foundation from
1964 to 1968, he was responsible for conferences and publications
in American Studies. Subsequently he became Professor of Art and
History at Lincoln University, the nation's oldest predominantly
Black institution. He also serves as Visiting Professor of Communica-
tions at Temple University.

In 1972 Dr. Fishwick was elected President of the Popular
Culture Association.

75977